Susan Glaspell's Century of American Women

SUSAN GLASPELL'S CENTURY OF AMERICAN WOMEN

A Critical Interpretation of Her Work

VERONICA MAKOWSKY

New York   Oxford
OXFORD UNIVERSITY PRESS
1993

Oxford University Press

Oxford   New York   Toronto
Delhi   Bombay   Calcutta   Madras   Karachi
Kuala Lumpur   Singapore   Hong Kong   Tokyo
Nairobi   Dar es Salaam   Cape Town
Melbourne   Auckland   Madrid

and associated companies in
Berlin   Ibadan

Copyright © 1993 by Oxford University Press, Inc.

Published by Oxford University Press, Inc.,
200 Madison Avenue, New York, New York 10016

Oxford is a registered trademark of Oxford University Press

Library of Congress Cataloging-in-Publication Data
Makowsky, Veronica A.
Susan Glaspell's century of American women : a critical
interpretation of her work / Veronica Makowsky.
p. cm.   Includes index.
ISBN 0-19-507866-7 (alk. paper)
1. Glaspell, Susan, 1876–1948 — Characters — Women.
2. Women and literature — United States — History — 20th century.
3. Heroines in literature.   I. Title.
PS3513.L35Z75   1993
818'.5209 — dc20   92-23329

1 3 5 7 9 8 6 4 2

Printed in the United States of America
on acid-free paper

For Joshua Jeffrey Gross
who provided the inspiration

Acknowledgments

I would like to thank Macmillan Publishing Company for allowing me to reprint the portion of Chapter 2 that appeared in their Scribner's *Modern American Women Writers*. I am grateful for a summer of research support from Louisiana State University. Karen Law, Mercedes Schneider, and Sigrid King have my admiration and gratitude as ideal research assistants.

Contents

Susan Glaspell's Century of American Women

Introduction:
The Hydra Heads of Obscurity

"Who *was* Susan Glaspell? Why are you working on *her*?" I am often asked. What my interlocutors really want to know is "If Susan Glaspell is so important, why haven't we heard of her? Why isn't she part of the literary canon?" These questions are valid and important; the answers tell us much about ourselves as critics and readers as well as much about Susan Glaspell. The answers are also complex; I cannot say that if one factor were different, Glaspell would be considered a major writer today. As Jane Tompkins has reminded us, "The reputation of a classic author arises not from the 'intrinsic merit' of his or her work, but rather from the complex of circumstances that make texts visible initially and then maintain them in their preeminent position.[1] Unfortunately, the reverse is also true: Glaspell's reputation was thwarted by a plethora of cultural and personal obstacles, the veritable hydra heads of literary obscurity.

Ezra Pound's poetic persona Hugh Selwyn Mauberley was troubled by what "the age demanded" of the artist. Mauberley, an aesthete, indicts the modern era:

> The age demanded an image
> Of its accelerated grimace,
> Something for the modern stage,
> Not, at any rate, an Attic grace;
>
> Not, not certainly, the obscure reveries
> Of the inward gaze;
> Better mendacities
> Than the classics in paraphrase![2]

Although Pound sympathizes with Mauberley's mysticism and Hellenism, he and his fellow international modernists were committed to "make it new," and to supply what they believed the age demanded, despite what the populace who comprised that age really wanted from art. In general, modernist works are difficult and purposely elitist: fragmented in form, dense with allusions, and despairing in tone; T. S. Eliot's *The Waste Land* is at once their anthem and their home. As readers and critics, founders or supporters of the literary canon, we have tended to accept the high modernists' version of what the age demanded, and so have neglected their contemporaries, such as Susan Glaspell (1876–1948), who wrote from an alternate tradition and with a markedly different sense of what the age demanded.

Glaspell was an idealist, a believer in truth and beauty, that "Attic grace" rejected by Pound. In contrast to the cosmopolitan modernists, she was a profoundly American writer in the transcendental tradition of Emerson and Whitman. Like them, she sought self-knowledge or truth in the often "obscure reveries of the inward gaze." In contrast with the despondent, elitist modernists, she shared Whitman's democratic optimism about the potential for human progress and so celebrated the so-called "common people," though she acknowledged their faults and the obstacles with which entrenched society confronted them.

In subject matter and style Glaspell also differed from the modernists. Sandra M. Gilbert and Susan Gubar have recently pointed out a missing element in the frequently cited influences upon modernism, "the profundity of the social metamorphoses brought about by the 'new women' and, in particular by their struggle for the vote."[3] Although not overtly political, Glaspell was a product of the era of the New Woman, approximately 1870 to 1920, and she wrote about women, their struggles for self-realization and their relationships with one another as well as with men. In this sense, she shares with the modernists an interest in what Gilbert and Gubar call "the battle of the sexes,"[4] though Glaspell concentrates on women's experiences and her heroines often manage to transcend this battle.

Glaspell's focus on women's experience, not the battle of the sexes, is an obvious cause of her literary obscurity and perfectly illustrates Dale Spender's vigorous indictment of women writers' dismissal by the overwhelmingly male literary establishment: "This has nothing to do with the quality of their writing—or the quality of the world they choose to depict—but is a value judgment, pure and simple, about their limited, inferior, and insignificant subject matter."[5] The "women's novel" has been a pejorative term for quite some time in American literary history, as attested by the envious Nathaniel Hawthorne's characterization of his popular contemporaries, those "damned scribbling women."

Glaspell and her ilk may be damned by Hawthorne and his successors for what they did, write about women and their lives, but she is also damned, in fame and sales, for what she did not do, namely, fit the paradigm of today's "women's novel," the supermarket romance novel, whether Harlequin or another brand, in which the heroine's ultimate goal is getting the hero to take care of her.[6] In contrast, Glaspell's heroines take responsibility for themselves and are able to nurture others, including men, only after they have achieved self-reliance.

Glaspell did not embrace Pound's dictum that the modern writer "make it new" in subject since women's trials are a very old story, nor did she do so in structure or in style, at least in her fiction, a choice of which Glaspell was quite conscious. Although she praised her modernist contemporary Virginia Woolf because she made "inner things real" and made "relationships realities as well as people," Glaspell's consideration for what a non-elite reading audience might enjoy caused her to reject Woolf's example. She wrote somewhat wistfully, "If one could have what she has, or something of it, and have also story, that simple downright human interest."[7] Her novels are generally conventional omniscient narrations with clearly comprehensible characterization, time schemes, and diction, and, of course, well-made, interesting plots. They are not fragmented, convoluted, allusive, or obscure; in short, they are generally quite easy and pleasant to read and readily convey Glaspell's beliefs. Inopportunely for her place in literary history, difficulty, not clarity, was valued by those exponents of modernism, the New Critics, who reigned in the academy well into the 1960s.

What reputation Glaspell has today can be credited to her plays, which are more radical and experimental, particularly *Trifles* (1916) and *The Verge* (1921). Ironically, instead of winning the praise of the drama critics of her day, her plays were often excoriated. Arthur Hobson Quinn's response to *The Verge* is typical. After summarizing it as "a study of a neurotic woman who is going insane," he points out its faults and a more appropriate model:

> The question remains, is the whole thing worthwhile? If there is one coherent idea in the play it is that only through violent suffering and wreckage of lives can any growth be attained. As this does not happen to be true the play fails the test of verity. After all, Susan Glaspell and Zona Gale [a contemporary playwright], keen as their love for the theatre may be, are more experimental than systematic in their work for it. This shows clearly when we contrast their achievement with the plays of an expert craftsman [Gilbert Emery] who devotes his entire attention to the theatre.[8]

After dismissing Glaspell's worldview as false, the Olympian Quinn tells us what is really wrong with Glaspell's work: it is written by a woman. He links her with another woman, Zona Gale, and uses "experimental" as a synonym for intuitive, a supposedly feminine quality which he opposes with the "systematic" or rational attributes of men. Glaspell and Gale were two highly professional writers, but Quinn casts them as dilettantes when he invidiously compares them to a man who apparently keeps his mind on business, "devotes his entire attention to the theatre," without the feminine distractions of men to serve as lovers or housekeepers.

"Experimental" is not always a pejorative term, especially when applied to Glaspell's fellow Provincetown Player, Eugene O'Neill, whose reputation vastly exceeded hers, even as novice playwrights. Another Provincetown Player and friend of Glaspell, Edna Kenton, remembered the summer of 1916 when Glaspell's husband, George Cram Cook, was "standing on the seabacked stage at Provincetown, telling me of the new great playwright to be, of the new great plays we were to produce."[9] That playwright with "new great plays" was, of course, Eugene O'Neill, not Cook's own wife Susan Glaspell.

Glaspell's relative obscurity today is partially related to her gender, but another form of prejudice is also responsible. Drama is in many ways the bastard child of American literature, grudgingly squeezed into an occasional college syllabus or segregated in an infrequent course on drama. If there is only room for one great playwright in the canon, it is the male O'Neill.

O'Neill was not the only man in whose shadow Glaspell dwelt. She was willingly subservient to her husband George Cram Cook, the founder and inspiration behind the Provincetown Players, and, after Cook's death, her lover Norman Matson, who is best known today for the novel that inspired the television series "Bewitched." Arthur and Barbara Gelb, O'Neill's biographers, describe Glaspell as "a delicate, sad-eyed, witty woman, [who] worshiped her husband and devoted herself in equal measure to him and to her writing; it was she who provided the backbone of their income."[10] Nilla, Cook's daughter by a previous marriage, recalled, "She subordinated herself completely, always to the man of the moment, was *anything* but a feminist, and always sad when work of her own succeeded more than my father's — or after, Norman Matson's."[11] Apparently, both men expected her, like *Bewitched*'s Samantha, to provide the mainstay of their lives, spiritually and economically, with a magical twitch of her nose.

All these obstacles were hydra heads for Glaspell's reputation but not for her accomplishment. In addition to her own sturdy self-reliance and persistence, Glaspell's work was facilitated by two nineteenth-century American literary traditions that were not prized by the pessimistic and elitist modernists, namely, transcendentalism and domestic fiction.

Glaspell's transcendentalism was the inspirational, not the chapter-and-verse, variety; it was the sort that was "in the air" in the late nineteenth century, rather than a meticulous culling of sources, so this account of her debt to the transcendentalists is necessarily generalized. She shared their belief in the ultimate goodness at the core of the universe and every human being. Emerson often called this goodness the Oversoul or Spirit, but he had a variety of names for it, as did Glaspell, who favored "beauty" and "truth." Although this may sound like romanticism in general, Glaspell's emphasis upon the necessity for nonconformity places her within the American transcendental tradition.

Since spirit dwells within each individual, his or her duty is to that spirit, not to social conventions. "Whoso would be a man, must be a nonconformist," said Emerson,[12] a pronouncement Glaspell would certainly emend to include women like Ruth Holland, the defiant heroine of her novel *Fidelity* (1915). If each individual were such a nonconformist and followed the spirit within him or her, Emerson believed that society would be reformed because it would be comprised of reformed individuals: "As fast as you conform your life to the pure idea in your mind, that will unfold its great proportions. A correspondent revolution in things will attend the influx of the spirit. So fast will disagreeable appearances, swine, spiders, snakes, pests, mad-houses, prisons, enemies, vanish."[13] Glaspell shared this belief about the means to social reform, but for her it was more a hope than a promise, as illustrated by the group of failed idealists in her novel *Norma Ashe* (1942). In addition, Emerson's demanding code was tempered for Glaspell with the democratic spirit and compassion for humanity, which Walt Whitman manifested in *Leaves of Grass*, and which imbues many of Glaspell's works such as her play *Inheritors* (1921) or her novel *Judd Rankin's Daughter* (1945).

Glaspell was fully aware of the justice of Emerson's comment that "for nonconformity the world whips you with its displeasure,"[14] but her works demonstrate that it more closely resembles assault with a deadly weapon where woman are involved. "I shun father and mother and wife and brother when my genius calls me. I would write on the lintels of the door-post *Whim*," Emerson blithely informs us.[15] In innumerable instances Glaspell's fiction and drama demonstrate how difficult a similar attitude is for women with their traditional obligations toward, as well as love of, their families and homes. She also realizes that they are more likely to be scrubbing the door-post than expressing themselves by carving upon it as artists. In her recognition of the peculiar difficulties faced by women in their quest for self-realization, Glaspell more closely resembles the transcendentalist Margaret Fuller, author of *Women in the Nineteenth Century*, and Glaspell often dramatizes many of the problems Fuller delineated in her essays.

Glaspell's models for her struggling, self-reliant women may well have been found in popular American nineteenth-century women's or domestic fiction. In *Women's Fiction: A Guide to Novels by and about Women in America*, Nina Baym outlines the basic plot of such novels: "It is the story of a young girl who is deprived of the supports she has rightly or wrongly depended on to sustain her throughout life and is faced with the necessity of winning her own way in the world."[16] Glaspell's heroines face similar reversals, though theirs may be loss of cherished beliefs as well as familial and economic deprivations. Glaspell's heroines also demonstrate the self-reliance that Baym notes in their precursors: they must find solutions for their own problems.[17] Finally, in many of Glaspell's novels, as in those Baym describes, "the men . . . are less important to the heroine's emotional life than the women,"[18] or for Glaspell, the heroine's exploration of herself.

Glaspell differs most from her nineteenth-century predecessors in the tentativeness of her happy endings. Baym describes endings that seem to realize Emerson's hopes for the reform of society through the reform of the individual, in this case, the individual woman: "The end of the change, finally, is a new woman and, by extension, the reformation of the world immediately around her as this new person calls out different relations and responses from her environment."[19] Glaspell's works do contain many examples of women whose moral superiority shames and inspires the men she saves by serving, such as the title character in her play *Bernice* (1919) or Frances "Blossom" Holt in her novel *Ambrose Holt and Family* (1931). In her mature works, however, her heroines' success is their ability to hope for a better world, not the achievement of that world, despite a few seemingly improved men. At the conclusion of Glaspell's novel, *Fugitive's Return* (1929), Irma Schraeder decides that "in her own vineyard would she labor,"[20] but we do not learn if her labors reach fruition. The title character of *Norma Ashe* manages to rekindle her idealism from the ashes of the waste land her life has become, but her circumstances do not improve.

Glaspell differs from much of this nineteenth-century fiction in her emphasis on mature woman as mother, not on young girl as daughter.[21] Indeed, Glaspell's treatment of maternity is particularly relevant to current debates within feminism. Some French feminists advocate a biological determinism since their theories derive from Freud (biology is destiny) by way of Lacan. Although they celebrate writing the body, they effectively relegate women to the private, nonverbal world of early infancy prior to the law or word of the fathers.[22] Glaspell's use of the maternal metaphor is closer to that of many American feminists, particularly the philosopher Sara Ruddick, in that maternity is not exclusively biological, but a way of viewing the world learned through loving and caring for children; it is not sentimental drivel but a philosophy that provides a basis for action within the world. What Ruddick calls "maternal thinking" is not limited to women or women who bear children, but is available to anyone, including men, who espouse this mode of thinking and feeling, though Glaspell's men rarely seem able to profit from it since they cannot look beyond themselves or their privileged positions in a male-dominated society. Most importantly, in Glaspell's work the benefits of "maternal thinking" are not restricted to the rearing of individual children, but promote the nurturance of humanity's potential for progress.[23]

The protagonist of Glaspell's *The Verge*, Claire Archer, is not interested in mothering her conventional debutante daughter. Instead Claire wishes to experiment with plants to create new and bolder life forms and keep her plants, and her life, on the risky but exciting "verge." Although both life and plants appear to be in ruins at the play's violent denouement, Glaspell suggests, in Claire's words from Act I, that although things "break themselves up into crazy things—into lesser things, . . . from the pieces—may come one sliver of life with vitality to find the future."[24] This is a pioneering, radical, adventuresome maternity, not the lulling comfort that we often associate with the term.

Claire Archer's maternity represents Glaspell's views taken to their extremes. A more typical example is found in her play *The Outside* (1917). Glaspell's two childless heroines live outside society at the end of the land on Cape Cod. In their nonconformity, they identify with the twisted, stunted vegetation near the water's edge. As one of them, Allie Mayo, comments, these "strange little things" are the necessary beginning of life and "hold the sand for things behind them. They save a wood that guards a town. . . . where their children live."[25] Glaspell's maternal metaphor is at once conservative and revolutionary. The women want to save what is best in the town, its future, progress in the form of the children, but Glaspell presents their unconventional lives and relinquishment of society's comforts as indications of the direction in which the future should go, toward the innovative, the original, the "outside."

For all these hopes, however, Glaspell's works demonstrate her awareness of the ways "oppression is largely responsible for the defects rather than the strengths of maternal thought," as Ruddick puts it. A mother may direct all her nurturance toward her own children in the spirit of cutthroat competition promoted by society as a whole, as does the title character of *Norma Ashe*. She may allow her children, particularly her sons, to domineer over the less privileged, as does Blossom Holt at the beginning of *Ambrose Holt and Family*.[26] Despite these temptations, as Blossom's later, more profound version of maternity illustrates, Glaspell's revisioning of motherhood can point the way for men as well as women to reinstate this concept in its beneficial, not stultifying, capacities.

Glaspell's works depict women's lives over a century of American history, from that of pioneers of the 1840s to war mothers of the 1940s, and I wish to examine her use of the maternal metaphor within this context. After a chapter on Glaspell's life that emphasizes the cultural background of her century of women, I proceed chronologically through her works. Since most of her work is out of print, I provide enough plot summary to make my analysis comprehensible to the reader. Perhaps this book can be regarded as one blow against the hydra heads of Glaspell's obscurity and a step toward making her works once more available for the pleasure and elucidation of the twenty-first century, new generations of readers, who are that future for which she longed and worked.

1

American Girl Becomes American Woman: A Fortunate Fall?

Susan Glaspell was at once blessed and cursed by the year of her birth. In 1876 the nation was celebrating its centennial, and, as Martha Banta reminds us, the American Girl became a primary symbol for the next three decades: "Many variations on the American Girl functioned actively at the turn of the century to represent a variety of ideals, but once the Girl became the symbol for the nation as a political entity, she was assigned as a strong image harboring explicitly imperialistic connotations."[1] While these "girls" in the popular press, advertisements, and art were presented as important and strong, their might did not arise from themselves, but from their infusion with the ideals of their culture. Significantly, it is an iconography of girls, not women, as befits the American worship of youth. When the appealingly venturesome girl becomes a wise and challenging woman, she is no longer the icon on the Liberty dime but the caricature of the threatening has-been, the smothering mother. Susan Glaspell's life is a remarkable illustration of such plaudits and plights for American women from 1876 to 1948.

Glaspell herself must have been quite conscious of the importance of the youthful or girlish image. Her literary biographer, Marcia Noe concludes that although Glaspell often asserted that she was born in 1882, the evidence actually points to July 1, 1876.[2] Glaspell's works attest her strong identification with America, yet she felt compelled to deny her birth during her country's centennial. Though she was, by all accounts, a kind, pleasant, attractive, competent, and talented woman, she felt a need to be considered younger than she was. What forces contributed to making this woman at once so capable and so vulnerable?

The United States celebrates its pioneer tradition. As befits a democracy, all pioneers are equal as they face the challenges of the wilderness. Glaspell's forebears were such rugged democrats who arrived in 1839 in what would become America's heartland, Iowa, near the Mississippi River. As the years passed, some became more equal than others, a theme she would explore through the impoverished childhood of the heroine of her novel *Fugitive's Return* (1929). In an autobiographical sketch, Glaspell characterized her family as struggling lower-middle-class and her education as public school.[3] Her self-deprecation indicates her consciousness of the failure of the American dream of a decent competence for all. Her youth was the era of the "robber barons" of the Gilded Age, and for their offspring, the melting pot of the public schools was no longer desirable.

Despite her realization that equality was an ideal more honored in rhetoric than in practice, Glaspell apparently received a decent education in the public schools where she began her creative writing. Although her family may not have been on the top rung of the social ladder, Glaspell herself seems to have overlooked these distinctions. "Old friends in her home town . . . recall the precocious, pretty little girl with a penchant for bringing home the ragged and hungry and making such queer friends in odd places."[4] Davenport could be enabling as well as supporting. Perhaps those "queer friends" were the children of the German and Irish immigrants who settled there in the bustling railroad and river town in the second half of the nineteenth century; these newcomers were instrumental to a cultural life that was impressive for a relatively small city: music societies, an art gallery, a museum, and literary and intellectual clubs.

Davenport was also the home of the novelist, Octave Thanet (Alice French), who may have provided Glaspell with a role model since Glaspell also did not marry or teach after her graduation from high school in 1894. Instead, she became a reporter for the *Davenport Morning Republican*, and then the society editor for

Davenport's *Weekly Outlook*. As Noe indicates, even her unconventional career of journalism was not enough, for "a frequent
theme in [her column] 'Social Life' is the dilemma faced by a girl
who has been brought up to reign at high-society events but has
come to see these occasions as superficial,"[5] a situation which
would also be faced by the heroine of her second novel, *The Visioning* (1911). Glaspell's intellect was not challenged by society teas,
so she entered Drake University in Des Moines, Iowa, in 1897.

Again, Glaspell's era at once enabled and handicapped her. The
last two decades of the nineteenth century and the first two of the
twentieth century are generally considered the era of the "New
Woman." The New Woman was reacting against woman's confinement in the home as prescribed by the nineteenth century's cult of
domesticity. The first generation of New Women, in the 1870s and
1880s, retained the ideal that women must serve others, but moved
their sphere of activity out of the home and into schools, settlement
houses, and other worthy public endeavors. Obviously, New
Women were not typical of the women of their day; they were a
plucky but privileged vanguard with the advantages of their race
and class, as well as what was perceived as their lack of ethnicity.
They helped their numbers increase by promoting the higher education of women so that, as Patricia Albjerg Graham states, "for a
brief period, from approximately 1875 to 1925, a strikingly hetero-
geneous array of acceptable and praiseworthy institutions existed
in America. This coincided with a crucial period in the history of
women in America and aided their advancement."[6] Drake University, founded as coeducational in 1881, was one of these institutions.

Others, however, questioned the consequences of women's edu-
cational advancement. Doctors and college presidents worried that
the blood that should be flowing to a woman's womb was being
misdirected to her brain, with dire consequences for her health and
the propagation of the race.[7] As Carroll Smith-Rosenberg observes, "College women were liminal figures locked together in a
novel ritual and a novel place. Conscious of being scrutinized by a
dubious world, they reached out to one another, forming the intense bonds of a shared identity that characterized the liminal experience."[8] At Drake University, Glaspell forged a similarly intense
bond to her lifelong friend Lucy Huffaker, with whom she engaged

in a friendly rivalry for various college offices and prizes. Their friendship and others Glaspell witnessed at Drake would reappear in her novel *Norma Ashe* (1942) as the bond between Norma and her friend Rosie, who tried to become the extraordinary women that college told them they would be in a world that prized only the ordinary, especially from women.

Glaspell made the most of her opportunities at Drake, as she had in her "public" education at Davenport. Marcia Noe describes her college years.

> She studied Greek, French, psychology, philosophy, history, and the literature of the Bible, accumulating a list of honors that included being chosen literary editor of the college newspaper, winning first prize in an oratorical contest in which she debated the subject of Bismarck and European politics, and participation in commencement exercises in June of 1899, contributing a short talk at the alumni banquet and a story at ceremonies held the previous day.[9]

This account is characteristic of Glaspell's energy, industry, enthusiasm, and curiosity. What was a woman to do with these qualities as she left the sheltered world of college and confronted turn-of-the-century America?

In many ways, Glaspell was typical of the second generation of New Women, as characterized by Smith-Rosenberg.

> Educated in the 1890s, often by the first generation of New Women, they came into their own in the years immediately preceding and succeeding the First World War. As political as the first generation, they placed more emphasis on self-fulfillment, a bit less on social service. . . . We see this as they moved into creative and artistic fields, and in their rejection of bourgeois sexual conventions. More at home in America's larger cities, they moved easily within the bohemian worlds of New York, Paris, and Berlin.[10]

Glaspell would later become involved with a married man and live unmarried with another; she would also join the bohemian world of New York's Greenwich Village, but her first startling act of nonconformity was taking a job as statehouse reporter, not society columnist, for the *Des Moines Daily News*.

In the masculine realm of journalism, Glaspell garnered knowledge of American democracy in action, which she would employ in her early short fiction. She also learned the discipline of her craft and years later wrote that the daily demands of newspaper work taught her that she could and must write, whether it suited her inclination or not.[11] Despite her professionalism, her column was called "The News Girl," and she also covered such events as the National Congress of Mothers. Her response to this gathering is an early indication of her definition of motherhood as helping the young, the future, even if these youth are not biologically one's own; Glaspell wanted "less time . . . spent in reading papers on altruism, etc., and passing biological resolutions and more of it . . . to looking after unbefriended children in their respective towns."[12]

In spite of her immersion in the capital's heady world of journalism, Glaspell's first love remained fiction. While at Drake, she had persisted in sending out stories in the face of rejections, and, in 1901, she went back to Davenport to devote all her energies to her fiction.[13] Glaspell's decision to return to home and the world of her imagination could be interpreted as an escape from the slings and arrows directed at a "girl" reporter or perhaps even women's fear of success. As Rachel M. Brownstein reminds us, "a literary genre without respectable classical ancestry, prose fiction was not defended from women, but rather, condescendingly, granted them."[14] Glaspell did not regard her choice of milieu and genre as a defeat, but wrote, "After less than two years of newspaper reporting I boldly gave up my job and went home to Davenport to give all my time to my own writing. I say boldly, because I had to earn my living."[15] Glaspell did not regard her fiction as a lady-like hobby or pastime, but a profession that demanded discipline and should command respect. In the decade after her graduation from college she placed over a dozen of her stories in such magazines as *Harper's* and *The Youth's Companion*.

As if her imagination had temporarily run dry after two years in Davenport, Glaspell went to Chicago in 1903 where she briefly attended graduate school in English at the University of Chicago. Her time in Chicago made an indelible impression upon her, for that city and its university appear as a mecca in both her early and late fiction. Under the innovative leadership of William Rainey Harper, the University of Chicago was becoming a major research institution in philosophy and sociology, attracting such figures as John Dewey. In his study of Chicago's literary world, Hugh Dalziel Duncan states:

> Between 1895 and 1910 the University of Chicago was a creative literary environment. James Weber Linn, Robert Morss Lovett, Donald Richberg, William Vaughn Moody, Edith Rickert, Robert Herrick, Norman Hapgood, Albion Small, and other university figures wrote novels, poems, plays, essays, and vital criticism of contemporary art.[16]

While these names no longer run trippingly from the tongue of the literary scholar, their bearers and their city believed themselves in the vibrant atmosphere of cultural ferment.

Duncan's list of literary luminaries also indicates that the University's creative atmosphere may not have been encouraging to everyone; successful women were experiencing backlash. Rosalind Rosenberg states that "by 1902 the enrollment of women had outstripped that of men, and many feared that within a few years, if nothing was done to prevent it, the university would become a woman's school."[17] During Glaspell's time there, women were once more fighting for their right to the same education as men and refused to be segregated in classes that were ostensibly separate but equal. They were led by the Dean of Women, Marion Talbot, who in her part of the 1902–1904 President's Report still had to defend women against charges that "they showed little inclination to pursue their studies in the graduate school" and that "women who pursue higher studies are not so persistent as men and their scholarship is not of so high a grade."[18]

Glaspell seemingly fulfilled this prophecy by once more returning to Davenport, but in her case because her metier was creative writing, not the dry historical scholarship typical of English departments at the turn of the century. The plight of women at the University was not lost on her, though. In *Norma Ashe* (1942), Glaspell's defeated heroine gazes wistfully at two young 1920s coeds who seem inappreciative of the education that was not available to her at the end of the nineteenth century.

In Davenport, Glaspell displayed what Marcia Noe calls "the conflicting aspects of her personality"[19] by spending Tuesdays with Davenport ladies at their study group, the Tuesday Club, while on

Sundays eschewing church in favor of the socialists and reformers of the Monist Club, where Glaspell said she found "the most interesting talk there had been in Davenport up to that time."[20] In this conflict, however, Glaspell's attempt at integration can be seen. Glaspell wanted the benefits of society: companionship, a sense of structure, a sense of the past; she wanted these positive aspects to continue into the better future to which the Monist Club was pointing. A smooth, gently upswinging curve was her ideal, not the wrenching motion of a pendulum, and in these early years, she and her fellow idealists believed it was possible, even for women.

In admittedly simplistic terms, there were basically two varieties of socialism at that time. The first was economic, based on Karl Marx's theories. An American exemplar is Philip Rappaport who wrote in 1906:

> Concrete matter existed prior to the abstract idea, and that, notwithstanding the force of moral ideas, there is a force of economic development in society working independent of moral ideas, and creating conditions, the influence of which is strong enough to alter, create and destroy moral ideas.[21]

The second, which I call the spiritually enthusiastic, held, like nineteenth-century American transcendentalism, that the progress of the material world was leading to a leap forward into the spiritual world. In his *What to Read on Socialism* (1906), Charles H. Kerr, head of a Chicago socialist publishing house, illustrates this idealistic vision.

> To feel one's unity with the universe, to find companionship with everything in and of the earth, to realize that this is not a chance world, but that all things have a cause, all contributing toward a cause; to know that man, of all beings, is the one which can consciously control and shape the forces throughout all to his good, this is inspiration indeed to the quickening soul. What a world it would be were every soul quickened with such inspiration![22]

It is not surprising to find that Kerr's reading list includes Whitman as well as Marx and Engels. Glaspell's socialism was of this latter variety because it supported her belief that matter and spirit or the individual and society were not opposed but were points on a progressive continuum.

Socialism may also have appealed to Glaspell because many, though not all, of its varieties espoused equality for women. Herbert Spencer argued that the properties of physical science, like evolution, could be applied to social and mental qualities as well. This progression could become regression for women since for Spencer progress entails increasing specialization and for women that means that their wombs are their most important organs, not their brains.[23] Others, like Glaspell, hoped that women could come into their own in a social order where brute force was no longer necessary but the "womanly" or maternal qualities of sharing and empathy would mitigate an industrial jungle.[24] In her *Women and American Socialism, 1870–1920*, Mari Jo Buhle states:

> The advent of machine production in the nineteenth century, Socialists and suffragists agreed, had fundamentally altered women's role by drawing large numbers of women into the work force and by simultaneously transforming the nature of the household itself. The major conclusion stood prominently: the political subordination of women was not merely unjust, as earlier women's rights advocates had argued, but no longer served the needs of modern society.[25]

Or, as socialist May Wood Simons more trenchantly expressed it in 1899, "Capitalism is no respecter of sex, but exploits men and women alike."[26] In any event, part of socialism's appeal for Glaspell would be the healing of one more schism or conflict; the battle of the sexes could end and complementary couples could march on to a better future.

In Glaspell's case, socialism had a personal as well as a humanitarian appeal because one of its exponents was Davenport's own George Cram Cook (1873–1924). In *The Road to the Temple* (1927), her biography of Cook, she wrote, "The Monist Society is important to me, for it was there I began to know Jig" (193–94). In the early years of this century, Davenport, however, did not share her enthusiasm for knowing him. Like his idol Henry David Thoreau, "Jig" Cook was censured for his apparent waste of a Harvard education, and also like Thoreau, for his refusal to teach school, in his case by resigning from Stanford University and the University of Iowa. In an era when divorce was by no means common, he had a second wife before he was thirty-five, and as if that were not affront enough, she was a feminist and anarchist. His rich and distinguished family could trace themselves back to the Revolutionary Minute Men and his father was a prominent railroad lawyer; the nonconformist Jig took up truck farming on his family estate, "the Cabin," outside Davenport as Thoreau had cultivated his beans on Emerson's land at Walden Pond. Also like Thoreau and the transcendentalists, although his way of life did not receive the locals' approbation, he did have his own coterie, the Monist Club and other intellectuals and seekers who would visit him at the Cabin.

By the time he met Glaspell, Cook had published three novels, some poetry, a history of his company during the Spanish American War, and some reviews. His interest in socialism had revolutionized his writing. G. Thomas Tanselle points out the difference between his novel of 1903, *Roderick Taliaferro* and his novel of 1911, *The Chasm*: "In 1903 Roderick Taliaferro, a heroic imperialist, enlisted the reader's sympathy on behalf of an established monarchy; eight years later Marion Moulton, a heroic revolutionary, draws the readers over to the side of the populace."[27] In his analysis of the two protagonists of *The Chasm*, Tanselle also illuminates an essential problem in Cook's worldview: "De Hohenfels is the Nietzschean with his theory that it is only out of an aristocratic few that a higher race of men can develop. . . , while Walt Bradfield, the socialist gardener. . . , is the earnest Marxist with his inflammatory soapbox speeches and his criticism of the superman doctrine."[28] If democrat is substituted for Marxist, these heroes represent Cook's life. He wanted to be one with the people, be they Iowa farmers, Provincetown fishermen, or Greek peasants, yet he was never content with them as they were, but felt compelled to lead them to a higher level. This tendency would also lead to his eventual split with the ostensibly democratic Provincetown Players amid charges of Cook's tyranny.

When Cook and Glaspell began to feel their mutual attraction, Cook was married to his second wife, Mollie Price, the feminist anarchist. At first, Glaspell was either too conventional or too considerate of another woman to pursue the relationship. The years 1909 to 1911 were interspersed with travels, first to Holland, Belgium, and France with her college friend Lucy Huffaker, financed by the success of her first novel, *The Glory of the Conquered*

(1909), and then to Colorado to visit a friend from Davenport, Mabel Brown, who was employed by the forest service. Davenport, and Cook, remained her magnetic point of return. She published two more books, a novel, *The Visioning* (1911), and her only collection of short fiction, *Lifted Masks* (1912).

By 1911, according to Marcia Noe, Glaspell had begun an affair with Cook despite the pregnancy of his wife. Cook, minus Mollie, moved to Chicago where he eventually became the assistant to his friend Floyd Dell on the *Friday Literary Review* of *The Chicago Evening Post*, which, Hugh Dalziel Duncan tells us, was "the 'intellectual paper' of Chicago" with "a brilliant staff of critics."[29] Glaspell joined Cook in Chicago, and on April 14, 1913, they were married in Weehawken, New Jersey. Since Glaspell was an established writer and independent woman of thirty-six, her attraction and subsequent marriage to the peripatetic and philandering Cook require some explanations.

Part of Cook's appeal for Glaspell was the way he could enact the rebellions that were more difficult for her because of her class and gender. She admired Cook's aristocratic indifference to public opinion and, in *The Road to the Temple*, contrasted it to her feelings of inferiority: "My own grandfather remained humbly on his fruit-farm—sheltered by no mansard roof, and had my clothes been jeered at on the street, my feelings would have been hurt" (10). Her shackling to the double standard was perceived by Cook who in 1907 wrote to Mollie of Glaspell, "Sweet as she is, she inspires such an attitude that to think of my kissing her is as though a devout Catholic should picture himself flirting with the Virgin Mary. Not but what it would be nice."[30] Cook himself was apparently devoid of such fetishes since he practiced free love in all three of his marriages.

Cook not only acted out rebellions for Glaspell, but supplied her with a reason, her great love for him, for breaking the bounds of convention and leaving the world of the Tuesday Club for that of Greenwich Village, the Monist Society writ large. In *Writing a Woman's Life*, Carolyn Heilbrun observes,

> In our own time of many possible life patterns, it is difficult to grasp how absolutely women of an earlier age could expel themselves from conventional society . . . by committing a so-

cial, usually a sexual, sin. The lives of women who died before
the middle of the twentieth century should always be carefully
examined for such an act, which would usually . . . occur in a
woman's late twenties or thirties.[31]

Glaspell seems an almost uncanny illustration of this pattern since
by marrying Cook she would no longer be the conventional, unmarried dutiful daughter of Davenport. She could realize what
Heilbrun calls the "unconscious decision to place one's life outside
the bounds of society's restraints and ready-made narratives."[32]

Glaspell, a productive professional writer, also perceived Cook's
less tangible and less consistent achievements as correspondingly
more authentic than hers. A close mutual friend, writer and socialist Floyd Dell, wrote of Cook, "It was not in written works, nor
even perhaps in deeds, but in that perishable substance, the memory of friends, that he left the full record of himself."[33] In *The
Road to the Temple*, Glaspell supplied similar rationalizations.

> Many so-called creative men have their radiant moment and then
> spend the rest of their lives realizing on that impulse of youth.
> Jig could not treat it like that, for he did not lose his youth. Life
> was a progress, a continuing belief, an ever-new dream. To 'cash
> in on' an old dream—no, the dream itself had been too fair, and
> what was left of life was too important (310).

Glaspell even justified Cook's frequent quests for transcendence
through inebriation. "A woman who has never lived with a man
who sometimes 'drinks to excess' has missed one of the satisfactions
that is like a gift—taking care of the man she loves when he has
this sweetness as of a newborn soul" (324). Through Cook, Glaspell
may have been attempting an early twentieth-century version of
"having it all," domestic affection without bourgeois conventions,
or, in other words, a way of maintaining the past's good with the
future's improvements.

Cook was less interested in continuity than in making new selves;
he saw himself as a free spirit as he moved from impulse to impulse, woman to woman, drunk to drunk. He could, of course, be
perceived as a selfish child since his behavior illustrates the difficulty of Emersonian self-reliance for other members of society who
believe in altruism, not simultaneous self-reliance, as the way to
improve the world. Although Glaspell may have seen herself as

barred from Cook's path by her gender, class, and innate kindness, her association with and nurturance of Cook made her the necessary link between the venturesome soul who promotes the future and the society that maintains the stability of the past; in short, she performed the function of a mother.

Both Glaspell and Cook used the maternal metaphor as the crucial bond between past and future. In *The Road to the Temple*, Glaspell quotes one of his early manuscripts: "Not without reason did the Christians paint Madonnas—mother and child on every chapel wall! For from the mother-love have sprung all loves. . . . He saw the age-long war all mothers wage with death" (116, 117). Although Glaspell was childless, mutual mothering was an important part of their relationship. If Glaspell nursed the hungover Cook like "a newborn soul," Noe tells us that "Jig babied Susan who had a heart lesion, back trouble, and various other real and imaginary illnesses."[34] One might argue that this reciprocal nurturing arose from Glaspell's inability to have children after a 1914 miscarriage; in *The Road to the Temple* she speculates that "perhaps it is true there was a greater intensity between us because of this" (239). Both Cook and Glaspell's uses of the maternal metaphor, however, actually predate their disappointed hopes of progeny and point to the importance of maternity in their philosophy.[35]

Glaspell gave much to Cook and they shared a great deal, but Cook also contributed to Glaspell's literary development. He introduced her to his brand of spiritual socialism, which was described by Floyd Dell:

> I remember hearing him tell of the *dipnoi*, those fish that were the ancient ancestors of man, coming out on dry land and breathing air, an element that burned like fire, and dying by countless millions before they had learned to breath it and live: and I saw in that story a symbol of the life of all forerunners, all who leave the familiar and go adventuring into strange regions of thought.[36]

Cook's influence and the model of his novel *The Chasm* are clearly indicated, if imperfectly digested, in Glaspell's *The Visioning* (1911). Several years later she applied Cook's progressive ideas to her own subject, the plight of an unconventional woman in society, and wrote what some consider her best novel, *Fidelity* (1915). The influence of Cook's specific ideas upon Glaspell is actually less important than the way he dared her to look beyond the conventional, a challenge that led to her greatest work, the radical plays she wrote for the Provincetown Players.

Cook had founded the Provincetown Players as part of his quest for a spiritual, intellectual, and material community. Many accounts have already been provided of the Players' founding, development, and eventual disintegration,[37] but for Glaspell, the changing of genre from fiction to drama became a liberating opportunity to overthrow convention in form as well as content. According to Glaspell, she owed that chance to Cook who, needing material for his first season, demanded that she write a play. She turned to a murder trial that she had covered in Iowa to produce the work for which she is best known today, her one-act play *Trifles*.[38] The genesis of *Trifles* is an excellent example of the way Glaspell could take an idea, or command, from Cook but make it valuable and her own by a fruitful union with her experiences.

From 1913 through 1922, Glaspell and Cook usually lived part of the year in Provincetown and part in Greenwich Village so that Glaspell had a supportive milieu of friends who were fellow intellectuals, socialists, radicals, and feminists. As June Sochen states in her history of feminism in Greenwich Village at that time, "Socialism, which accepted feminism as a plank in its official platform, was the Village's pervasive philosophy."[39] In this congenial atmosphere, Glaspell could experiment with the radical feminism of the play that many consider the highlight of her oeuvre, *The Verge* (1921). These years were productive in quantity as well as quality since she wrote eleven plays of varying lengths, including two in collaboration with Cook. Significantly, she published no novels from *Fidelity* in 1915 until *Brook Evans* in 1928. This fictional drought may be explained by the demands of the Provincetown Players and then a sojourn in Greece that began in 1922, but it is important to note that Glaspell was always highly attuned to her audience. Her fiction was directed at a more traditional audience, the readers of domestic or women's novels, not the Village "bohemians," and her goal was enough money for a living, not experimentation.

The Provincetown years seem mainly happy ones for Glaspell. She was intensely creative, she was valued by many interesting friends, and she had a house on Cape Cod that she loved. Her disappointment at her inability to bear children was somewhat mitigated by the enjoyable visits of Harl and Nilla, Cook's children by his second wife. Even the difficulties of living with the impulsive Cook seemed more an invigorating challenge than a burden during this charmed period.

All this changed as Cook, supported by Glaspell, gradually and often vituperatively, severed his ties with the Provincetown Players because he believed they were becoming too commercial by directing their efforts toward Broadway. In addition, the heady atmosphere of the earlier Village was stifled by the entry of the United States into World War I and by the Red Scare of 1919. The incorrigibly restless and questing Cook, however, may simply have become bored with the status quo and stifled by success, and so needed to move forward to the next experience. Thoreau left his famous experiment at Walden Pond because "it seemed to me that I had several more lives to live, and could not spare any more time for that one."[40] Cook wanted to proceed to his next life where he could fulfill his aspiration to become a Greek Thoreau, so he and Glaspell sailed for Greece on March 22, 1922.

The trouble is that what may have been a renewal for Cook was an uprooting for Glaspell. While Cook wrote many of the poems that Glaspell later collected in *Greek Coins* (1925), Glaspell seemed to be in a creative drought since she did not publish any more novels until 1928 or plays until 1931. Glaspell's intense identification with her Midwestern and American background left her deracinated in Greece, despite her interest in its monuments, its scenery, and especially its people. One must also note that the traditional society of Delphi, where they eventually settled, was a patriarchy. While the "Kyria" was respected, the "Kyrie" was the important one.

In Greece, Glaspell felt compelled to become the supporting player in what was Cook's greatest role, his attempt to become Greek in spirit as well as dress. If Cook was drinking with the local men in the wineshops, Glaspell was at home alone. If his visiting daughter Nilla was experiencing adolescent angst, Glaspell should cope with it. If in the spring Cook wanted to move with the villagers up the mountain with their flocks, Glaspell joined him in vulnerability to bandits and the rigors of living in a hut. Significantly, they had separate huts because as Cook became increasingly a different, Greek, person, he seemed to be rejecting Glaspell as a part of a cast-off earlier life. Unlike Glaspell, Cook refused to accept mature love as different from, but not necessarily inferior to, the passion of youth. In *The Road to the Temple*, Glaspell recalled a conversation with Cook: "After years together, something goes, yet is it all loss? Does not something also come? He did not care for that way of looking at it, he said. He was the lover" (388). And what was Glaspell to be without her role of beloved?

Glaspell's trip to Iowa in the winter of 1922–23 may have provided a respite from this increasingly untenable situation as well as a chance to visit her sick and widowed mother, but the resolution came with Cook's death on January 14, 1924 of the glanders he had contracted from a pet dog. As was appropriate for the person he had become, he was buried at the temple of Delphi in full peasant regalia. In February, Glaspell returned to her native soil without him, and she could finally mourn the loss which she had, in a sense, experienced before his death.

Despite their marital problems in these last years, Glaspell was devastated by Cook's death. She attempted to come to terms with it by editing Cook's poems in *Greek Coins* (1925) and writing his biography, *The Road to the Temple* (1927). After a relatively slight novel, *Brook Evans* (1928), which did treat the theme of expatriation, she completed her mourning by imagining modes of solitude in her next two novels. In *Ambrose Holt and Family* (1931), an outwardly conformist but inwardly rebellious heroine learns to keep her convictions despite society; she wants to assist her poet husband through the example of a wandering wise man, her husband's father, who had abandoned family obligations but died at peace with himself and others. Cook is found here in the portraits of husband and father, suggesting how much Glaspell felt she had lost. In *Fugitive's Return* (1929), a heroine stricken dumb with grief finds her voice at Delphi by listening to the oracle within herself, not the articulations of men, and attempts to complete her cure by resolving to live independently in America.

Glaspell herself was less able to sustain such self-reliance. After her return to the United States in February 1924, she seemed at loose ends and drank more compulsively. The America to which she returned was no longer a haven for socialism and feminism, but a playground for the hedonism of the roaring twenties. The "new" women of the previous era had actually returned to their old role as playthings. Carroll Smith-Rosenberg writes:

The New Man could portray the New Woman as the enemy of
liberated women because he had redefined the issue of female
autonomy in sexual terms. He divorced women's rights from their
political and economic context. The daughter's quest for pleasure, not the mother's demand for political power, now personi-
fied female freedom.[41]

Glaspell found herself alone in this not-so-brave new world where
her age made her one of the outmoded mothers, not the sex-object
daughters.

In the autumn, Robert Frost's oven bird asked "what to make of
a diminished thing,"[42] but at nearly fifty, Glaspell seemed to be
asking how to repeat in her life's autumn the things of its spring,
however diminished. She took up with another writer who needed
nurturing, the novelist Norman Matson, who was some seventeen
years her junior. As she had twice with Cook, Glaspell collaborated
once with Matson on a play, *The Comic Artist* (1928). Like Cook,
Matson was not her equal in literary accomplishment since his
lasting achievement seems to have been the novel that inspired
the television series *Bewitched*, and he did not even have Cook's
compensatory ability to engage the talents of others. Nor was he
able to maintain his convictions as Cook did, however extremely;
by 1934 Matson was mocking his liberal-left past in the conservative *American Review*.[43]

In what was less a union of mystical beliefs than of mutual
comforts, Glaspell and Matson enjoyed nature, pets, and trips to
Norway, the American Southwest, Mexico, England, and France,
but they did not share a marriage certificate. Although Glaspell
had defied convention to love the married Cook, she and Matson
lived together without matrimony but allowed others to think they
were married. Glaspell said she did not want to distress her failing
mother with the truth, but the fact that Glaspell did not want
Matson to visit her mother's home with her, even if he were in the
region, may indicate that she did not really want to be seen in
Davenport, or see herself as, a wife to a lesser man than Cook.[44]

Even the dissolution of her relationship with Matson seems a
pathetic version of her earlier troubles with Cook, for Matson was
an egotist on a more petty scale. He told Glaspell that he was
unable to live in the shadow of her success or on her money. As
Glaspell's health worsened and she lost more and more teeth, he

reinforced the message of the older woman's worthlessness in America's youth culture by leaving her in 1932 to marry a nineteen-year-old who would bear him the child Glaspell could not.

As the United States became sunk in the Depression, so Glaspell was thoroughly swamped in her own malaise throughout the thirties. Perhaps in another attempt to relive an earlier, happier time, she turned to the theater. *Alison's House* (1930), based on the life of Emily Dickinson, is not the sort of radically experimental play Glaspell was writing more than a decade before, and it won the Pulitzer Prize for Drama in 1931. Glaspell also tried to reprise the creation of community and the nurturance of talent that she and Cook had known with the Provincetown Players when she became Midwest Director for the Federal Theater Project from 1934 to 1935. She served ably, but the experience was not that of her heady earlier years, and she returned to Cape Cod to her many friends and her garden.

Despite financial strains, a drinking problem, failing vision, and generally deteriorating health, Glaspell identified with her country's role in the 1940s and was exhilarated by the increasing value of a woman's work outside the home. She supported the fight against fascism in the Second World War through writing articles and speaking, creating a children's book, cultivating her liberty garden, and even contributing to the metal drive the bronze plaque honoring Cook's role in the Provincetown Players.

Glaspell's late fiction is uneven in quality but intensely moving in its re-evaluation of her life and ideals and those of her country. *The Morning is Near Us* (1939), *Norma Ashe* (1942), and *Judd Rankin's Daughter* (1945) all treat the struggle of subjugated daughters to become empowered and empowering mothers, not of biological children, but of a better future. As the horrors of the era increased, Glaspell's heroines struggled to keep the faith, but that faith also appeared an increasingly diminished thing in the looming, encroaching darkness, which also claimed Glaspell, who died of viral pneumonia on July 28, 1948. Perhaps it is fitting that a life so closely identified with that of her country, particularly its women, should close before women's role had come full circle, and they were once more encased in the domestic sphere, relegated to suburban enclaves in the 1950s version of the cult of domesticity.

2

The Glory of the Conquered: Cultural Confusions and Apprentice Fiction

In the early years of the century, Susan Glaspell began her successful career as a writer of popular short fiction, and, like most novices, she wrote from her own experience. Many of her early stories treat the world of state politics, which she had covered for the *Des Moines Daily News* as the "News Girl." Some of these were later collected in *Lifted Masks* (1912), which, as Marcia Noe remarks, "is appropriately titled, for the typical protagonist of her early fiction is a sort of closet idealist who 'comes out' to reveal an inner core of integrity under a cynical exterior when he approaches his Moment of Truth."[1] These idealists are generally male politicians or other public figures, and though their epiphanies are occasionally precipitated by women, the men hold center stage, as in "The Intrusion of the Personal" (1904) or "For Tomorrow" (1905).[2]

Glaspell also mined her personal experience as a small-town girl who tries to succeed in the big city, the Chicago of 1903 where she did some graduate work. In these stories, Glaspell uses her feelings of alienation and anxiety to explore themes that would become prominent in her mature work: the difficulties of sisterhood in a world where female identity is established by competing for males and the conflict between a woman's art and her life. These themes find a tentative, sometimes strained, resolution in her emerging view of the female artist as a mother-figure who nurtures humanity's soul and so transcends the conflicts between women and between a woman's gendered identity and her art. This chapter examines some of these stories about women and their thematic culmination in Glaspell's first novel, *The Glory of the Conquered: The Story of a Great Love* (1909).[3]

In two stories that were published in the *Youth's Companion*, "The Girl from Down-Town" (1903) and "The Boycott on Caroline" (1906), the difficulties of sisterhood are presented somewhat blatantly, as one might expect from the audience.[4] "The girl from down-town" is actually a young woman from the country, Millie, who is clerking at a large urban department store. She wishes to move near the University and the lake, "away from the room where she could not look out, and from those girls whose way of laughing bothered her" (160). She rents a room, but is asked to move out by the University women who board there so that a former housemate can have her room. The former housemate realizes her false position as a woman who wants to work at a settlement house but cannot live with someone from a lower class, and so offers to share the room with Millie. Although this appears to be a happy ending in which snobbery and hypocrisy are vanquished by sisterhood, it actually promotes those vices. If a young woman prefers the quieter, or more repressed, ways of University women to those of lower-class women whose "way of laughing bothered her," she can be accepted into the group, but the mores of the upper class remain the standard by which all are judged.

Similarly, "The Boycott of Caroline" reveals a Glaspell who remains oblivious to her class prejudices. Caroline Stuart's family has moved to a new town where she is mystified by her snubbing by five girls whom she thought would be her friends. One of the girls, Marion, had "read a story about some people who were 'vulgarly rich'" (137), and so she affixes that label to Caroline in order to add some drama to the decorous dullness of Elmwood. The misunderstanding is cleared away when Marion finds Caroline in tears and decides she is one of them. Presumably if Caroline had been what Marion considers "vulgar," she would justifiably have been excluded from the group. Glaspell reinforces the values of her upper-middle-class audience in that sisterhood is represented as exclusive sorority, but even this limited sisterhood is possible only because these adolescent women do not yet have men as sources of contention.

In contrast, "Contrary to Precedent" (*Booklover's Magazine* 1904) examines feminine rivalry in a world that assigns a woman's status according to that of her mate.[5] Mrs. Kramer has been betrayed many times by her philandering husband Charlie, and she wants revenge. When she discovers some love letters written to her husband by an idealistic, artistic local girl, Christine Holt, she believes she can gain recompense for her years of suffering. She cultivates Christine's friendship, but only in order to make her eventual ultimatum even more brutally shocking: she tells Christine that she must recall her newly accepted first book from her publishers or she will tell Christine's fiance, Oscar Fairchild, about the letters. At first, Christine elects to recall the book, but later concludes that the book means too much to her and decides to take her chances with Mrs. Kramer and Oscar. When Mrs. Kramer confronts Oscar, she finds herself incapable of completing her revenge since she sees her earlier, happier self in Christine.

This somewhat overwrought plot reveals the techniques, images, and themes of Glaspell's later dramatic masterpieces. In a curious bit of self-reflection, Glaspell has Christine see her situation as "a rather cheap, melodramatic play" (235) and wonder if "the scene would be very effective" (236). Glaspell herself attempts a scenic method; instead of editorial moralizing, she uses dialogue and suggestive gestures, such as Mrs. Kramer's fingers nervously twisting a growing vine as she would like to warp and destroy the younger woman (236). The menaced and menacing vine would recur in Glaspell's innovative play, *The Verge* (1921).

Such small gestures also prefigure the importance of "trifles" in Glaspell's 1916 dramatic masterpiece by that name. Through Christine, Glaspell works out her theory of drama. As she contemplates life as a play, Christine perceives "the outward commonplaceness of things that were tragic" (244) and believes that "which she had read in books was wrong. At crucial times people acted just as they did in the commonplace hours — really they acted more so. And that would be a good feature to bring out in the play. The tragedy of the play must be very quiet, very conventional, and commonplace" (236).

The story also examines one of Glaspell's major themes, the conflict between a woman's desire for the comforts of heterosexual love and the challenge of personal integrity through art as epitomized by Christine's choice between her fiance and her book: "the primitive woman of her . . . , that essentially human in her heart which called out for love as the thing she could not do without" (243), wants to recall the book from the publisher, but Christine ultimately chooses the book, which she equates with "her soul, herself" (247). Glaspell's heroines usually make this, the "right" choice, always at the cost of pain and deprivation, but they never pay as much as a woman like Mrs. Kramer, who has numbed "her soul, herself" for a social concept like marital vengeance.

As so often in Glaspell's work, men may be a source of conflict between women, but in many ways they are not major characters. They are childish: Mrs. Kramer's husband is a good-time "Charlie" and Christine's fiance is Oscar, the "Fair-child." Since men need mothering, women become enablers who allow them to function in the world. In *19th-Century American Women's Novels*, Susan K. Harris finds that this mothering of mates is

> a code describing a major strategy American women use to maintain themselves and their marriages when they discover that their husbands are not equal to them. In a society in which divorce was shameful, a viable way to cope with a man who could not or would not rise to his wife's level of intelligence, morality, or courage was for her to assume a stance that admitted intimacy but at the same time preserved distance and respect; that is, to act as his mother.[6]

"Contrary to" the "precedent" of her nineteenth-century predecessors, Christine selects a different progeny when she finds herself "patting the sheets of paper [her book] much as though she were soothing an injured child" (247). Although Christine's choice appears preferable to indulging overgrown boys, it too may be an evasion. As Margaret Homans points out in *Bearing the Word*, "to define writing as motherhood holds out the possibility of justifying the woman writer's temerity by neutralizing the conflict between writing and motherhood."[7] For the turn-of-the-century woman, damned if you do and damned if you don't.

Despite these excursions into the opposition between heterosexuality and art, Glaspell's major theme in "Contrary to Precedent" is the limited and vicarious consolation of mothering a daughter in a world that provides women only with Hobson's choices. The older woman's spirit, deadened by years of pain, is resurrected by a younger woman in whom she sees her vanished self. Her soul is revivified, first by the negative emotion of jealousy, but then by a vision of maternity. As she gazes into the fire, Mrs. Kramer sees "the suffering faces of women, she could see the white hands reached out in imploration, and she could see the open, bleeding hearts" (251), so that, contrary to the precedent of women battling over men, she cannot complete her revenge. Maternity here may be an evasion of sisterhood, but it may also be a means of transcendence; if you take the higher ground, you can avoid confronting your rival-equal-sister under the terms dictated by masculine egos.

Art, of course, can be another version of this higher ground, but it remains inextricably linked with maternity in three of Glaspell's early stories, "The Return of Rhoda" (*Youth's Companion* 1905), "At the Turn of the Road" (*Speaker* 1906), and "For Love of the Hills" (*Black Cat* 1905).[8] Again, it appears in its baldest form in the story written for an adolescent audience. Rhoda returns from the city to her country home after learning that she would never become a great singer because she has only "a nice little home voice" (40). After her tears, Rhoda sings for her parents, "there's no place like home" (40). In the midst of this sentimental triteness, Glaspell does interject an interesting twist when Rhoda cries, "Our dream's gone, mother!" (40). An artistic failure becomes a maternal failure in that Rhoda's mother had not somehow supplied the wherewithal to make the dream a reality, but, more importantly, the daughter's artistic failure is a failure to provide her mother with the means to live vicariously through her daughter. For these women, the platitude that "there's no place like home" ironically indicates a promised land outside domesticity to which the daughter's artistry was to have provided admission for both women.

Admission to this promised land is granted to the heroine of "At the Turn of the Road" who is studying art in Chicago. She lacks the money to go home to Des Moines for Christmas since she is "living for the future—sacrificing for it" (360). In the public library, she turns to the Des Moines newspaper for solace. There she meets a man who has made money, "but after years of isolation—consecration you may call it, it you like—one loses the capacity for friendship . . . the human heart was not made to feed on gratified ambition" (360–61). He gives her the money to go home for Christmas so that she can avoid his mistake: "You'll paint your pictures all right, I'm sure of that—you have the look of success in your eyes; but I want you to hold on to the other things too" (361). This story is a pure fantasy, a wish-fulfillment in that a major source of the female artist's oppression, a capitalist patriarch, turns into Santa Claus and allows her to have it all, a personal life and an artistic career.

"For Love of the Hills" presents a successful resolution of the problems presented in "The Return of Rhoda" and "At the Turn of the Road." A young woman from Colorado goes to Chicago to try to find work that will pay for her art classes at night. She is down to her last eleven dollars and "enlisted in Chicago's great army of the homesick" (1) when she too turns for comfort to the public library's copy of her local newspaper. There she meets an elderly woman who longs to see the Colorado mountains once more before she becomes completely blind. The young woman collects enough money to send the older woman to the mountains, and she did so through the potency of her art: "she told the story with the simpleness of one speaking from the heart, and the directness of one speaking to those sure to understand" (9). Unlike Rhoda, she provides for the needs of her mother-figure, in effect, acting as a mother to one whose age and disability make her as vulnerable as a child. Successful artistry is successful maternity because maternal feelings lead to true art, a seemingly charmed circle.

What, though, makes admission to this charmed circle possible? In two works of 1909, "From A to Z" and *The Glory of the Conquered*, Glaspell attempts to answer this question by presenting a failed applicant, Edna Willard, and a triumphant one, Ernestine Hubers.[9]

In "From A to Z," University of Chicago graduate Edna Willard dreams of a career in publishing, but the job she obtains leaves her no scope for creativity or initiative. She must paraphrase definitions for a "new" dictionary with men who had failed in other careers from "age, dissipation, antiquated methods" (80). One such man, Clifford, the former editor of a great city newspaper, has the desk next to hers. Edna is attracted by his voice, one that "the prince used to have in long-ago dreams" (76). She tries to pursue their acquaintance, but he rebuffs her, ostensibly chivalrously, because of his ongoing battle with alcoholism. When the dictionary at last arrives at Z, she wants to try to reach him one more time, but she cannot bring herself to do so. A note that he has left her spurs her to follow him to his lodgings, but on the way she feels terribly ill and is found by her paternalistic beau, Harold, who tells her that "the place for you to-night is home. I'm taking you where you belong" (99).

Edna's society leaves her no outlet for her creativity. As a woman she only qualifies for a job with publishing's male dregs where her originality will be safely suppressed. Since creativity and maternity are virtually synonymous for Glaspell, Edna redirects her energy into mothering Clifford, who at first seems a promisingly vulnerable object since "he seemed always to know just what she was trying to say; he never missed the unexpressed" (82). In other words, he appears to possess what society defines as a woman's gift of sensitivity toward the feelings of others; he has been further emasculated by his failure as an editor and his dependency on alcohol. In contrast to Harold's oppressively robust masculinity, Clifford's feminization seems to make him less of a threat to Edna's potential as an autonomous person. Understandably, Edna does not seem to consider equality an option in this gender-ridden milieu.

Although Clifford seems to be a fellow repressed artist, he is actually as obtuse as Harold. When Clifford first kisses Edna, "he held her fiercely. . . . He frightened her. He hurt her. And he did not care — he did not know" (92). He imagines her as a goddess of domesticity, "sitting before a fireplace as symbolising the warmth and care and tenderness and the safety that will surround you" (95). Worst of all, he devalues her mind by defining womanhood as a disease that learning failed to cure: "They made a grand failure of you out at your university; they taught you philosophy and they taught you Greek, and they've left you just as much the woman as women were five thousand years ago" (94).

Obviously, Clifford wants to believe that Edna is more of a failure than he is in order to boost his own ego, but this is not evident to Edna who only observes, "Perhaps men never understood women" (96). Her subconscious ambivalence about pursuing him is indicated by her vacillation at the office and her sudden illness on the way to his lodgings, but she does consciously choose self-sacrificing, thankless nurturing when she follows him. In her study of nineteenth-century American domestic novelists, Mary

Kelley observes that "the insistent, urgent presentation of woman as the glorified, ultimate practitioner of the ethic of selfless service stood instead as a transparent shield overlaying an always dependent and vulnerable figure."[10] And so it is here: as Edna returns home with Harold, she realizes the force of circumstances and society in an almost deterministic or Darwinian fashion.

> Did things like rain and street-cars and wet feet and a sore throat determine life? Was it that way with other people, too? Did other people have barriers — whole cities full of them — piled in between? And then did the Harolds come and take them where they said they belonged? Were there not *some* people strong enough to go where they wanted to go? (100).

In *The Glory of the Conquered*, Glaspell answers that question in a sort of *bildungsroman* of the superwoman Edna is not.

Initially, Ernestine Stanley does not seem a prominent candidate for a new kind of heroine since her parents are stereotypical embodiments of nineteenth-century gender roles. Her father, a professor of biology, "believed only in that which could be reduced to a formula" (5), while her mother writes poems that were "not the songs of a poet at all; they were but the helpless reaching out of an unsatisfied, unanchored soul" (9). Their worldviews were so different that they could not agree on a name for their daughter until she was ten years old when they selected "Ernestine" through a comic juxtaposition of associations. "Her father approved it for what it meant in the dictionary; — her mother for the music of its sound" (5). Neither, however, realizes what her name will signify: one who can combine in earnest the strength and reasoning associated with masculinity and science with the sensitivity and creativity relegated to femininity and art.

In order to achieve this synthesis, Ernestine must first mature, which in Glaspell's view means moving from girlhood to motherhood. Carroll Smith-Rosenberg describes the two roles socially prescribed for nineteenth-century women: "The True Woman was emotional, dependent, and gentle — a born follower. The Ideal Mother, then and now, was expected to be strong, self-reliant, protective, an efficient caretaker in relation to home."[11] A woman was supposed to leap miraculously from one to the other or schizophrenically maintain both roles at once. Glaspell shows Ernestine moving from True Girl-Woman to the Ideal Mother, but in a progression impelled by maturity and experience, not a magical transformation.

During her courtship and newlywed years, though, Ernestine seems destined to repeat her mother's role. Her suitor, research scientist Karl Hubers, calls her "little one" (11) and "poor little girl" (12). Ernestine acquiesces in this childish role during Karl's "proposal": "He had not *asked* her to marry him. He had simply come and told her she *was* to marry him. And he was a great, strong man — far more powerful than she. She had positively nothing to do with it!" (4). As Janice A. Radway points out in her study of popular romance novels, because the hero "finds her irresistible, the heroine need not take any responsibility for her own sexual feelings. She avoids the difficulty of choosing whether to act on them or not."[12]

Karl takes Ernestine's cue and regards the loss of their first and only infant as an occasion to continue infantilizing Ernestine: "It was as a child she had been to him in those days, and he had comforted her as one would comfort an idolised child, whose hurt one strove to take wholly unto one's self" (34). As he notes later, "he loved this child in her" (78). If, as Glaspell often implies, mothering is the highest way of relating to another, what could be wrong with Karl's mothering Ernestine? Mothers, by definition, endeavor to help children to grow, to achieve their potentials, but Karl wants Ernestine to remain a child.

Ernestine can grow beyond her "little-girl" role because of a combination of her innate qualities and her circumstances. Unlike her parents who have such difficulty compromising, Ernestine believes in love, the force which Glaspell thinks moves humanity forward. To Ernestine at the time of her marriage, "all that was wrong in the world came through too little loving. All that was great and beautiful came from love which knew not doubts nor fears. . . . Love would deal kindly with her own" (10). Ernestine is obviously naive, and the rest of the novel indicates that love is not kind to its own, yet the novels' subtitle is *The Story of a Great Love*. Ernestine needs to learn that love is not an external force that determines her fate, but a force she can control and use for the highest purposes.

Despite her naivete, Ernestine, like her creator, can see beyond the conventional romance plot that ends with the union of hero and heroine.

> So many things in literature stop short when the people are married. I think that's such an immature point of view — just as if that were the end of the story. And when they write stories about married people they usually have them terribly unhappy about having to live together, and wishing they could live with some one else. It seems to me they leave out the best part (82).

Glaspell does put in "the best part," Karl and Ernestine's love for each other, but she depicts it as growing through trial, not remaining the stagnant "and they lived happily ever after" that Ernestine believes possible.

Glaspell demonstrates that Ernestine can grow beyond her conventional gender role because she is a true artist. As a child, drawing on the blackboard "seemed the only thing which made her all one" (6). When she describes a planned painting to Karl, she says that the young woman in it has dropped her book and is drinking in the grandeur of nature. Karl suggests that the woman's eyes should be closed, but Ernestine replies, "I think not. It seems to me she must be open to it in every way to make it stand for life, in the sense I want it to" (144). Ernestine can oppose Karl when it comes to her art, and she wants the woman in her painting to appear strong, capable of confronting experience instead of hiding from it. Ernestine's art is characteristic of her era, for, as Martha Banta states, in paintings of this period, "strong images of women are not necessarily of women engaged in forms of work. Portraits of women who live for the time being within their minds or their unconsciousness may in fact be portraits of women doing useful work."[13]

Glaspell also indicates that Ernestine is a genuine artist by providing her with a foil, Karl's cousin Georgia McCormick. At first Georgia seems a much stronger and more modern woman because she supports herself in the rough-and-tumble world of urban journalism. Later in the novel, she surprises many, Ernestine included, by giving up her career to marry a paper-bag millionaire. Glaspell suggests that Georgia is making the right decision when she tells Ernestine about newspaper work:

> It's thankless. And you never get anywhere. You break your neck one day, and then there's nothing to do the next, but start in and break it again. You're never any better to-day for yesterday's killing. Now with you—when you paint a good picture, it stays painted (230).

As did Edna Willard in "From A to Z," Georgia knows the difference between hackwork and art; also like Edna, she rejects the violent competition of "break[ing]" and "killing" for the security of domesticity. Edna and Georgia do not have Ernestine's options because they do not have Ernestine's talent and drive. Glaspell did, and she left journalism to devote herself to fiction.

Glaspell's portrait of the artist as a young woman is part of a cultural reconsideration of the relationship of women to art. Elaine Showalter indicates the difference between the Victorian and modern conceptions of women and careers: "Nineteenth-century feminists did not see marriage and public life in conflict for women; they recognized them as mutually *exclusive*," as did Georgia. "To be modern," as Ernestine aspired to be, "meant to want heterosexual love as well as work; neither was sufficient by itself," according to Showalter.[14]

As Mary Kelley demonstrates in *Private Woman, Public Stage: Literary Domesticity in Nineteenth-Century America*, these domestic novelists claimed to write in the privacy of their homes in order to obtain the money to support those domestic sanctums. In contrast, in her book on turn-of-the-century American women writers, Elizabeth Ammons states:

> While the tradition of domestic writers continued (as it does to the present day), especially among popular writers, most of the authors I am talking about either consciously broke with that heritage or never identified with it, declaring in the ways they lived their lives, in the statements they made about themselves as writers, and in the work they produced, that they were determined to be artists.[15]

Although Ammons does not consider Glaspell in her book, the definition fits, with the exception that the women whom Ammons discusses were more interested in exploding conventional form and technique than Glaspell, or, for that matter, Ernestine Stanley.

In this, her first novel, though, Glaspell still seems close to her nineteenth-century female predecessors despite some of the trappings of modernity. Glaspell wants Ernestine to "have it all," in the modern feminist sense, but she makes Ernestine earn it all through pain and suffering in accordance with the nineteenth-century sentimental Christian paradigm. Like that of the nineteenth century's feminized maternal Christ, Ernestine's "crucifixion" is a sign of her ultimate triumph, "the glory of the conquered." The title refers to a sculpture by Antoine Mercié, the "Gloria Victis," of which the Hubers own a reproduction, Ernestine's "favourite bronze" (47), and it is reproduced on the cover and the title page of the novel. A swooning winged male with a broken sword is supported by a strong-looking maternal figure, obviously a kind of Pieta. One does not have to be a zealous Freudian to realize that the woman is glorious because she now has more power than the impotent male.[16] The classic nineteenth-century literary example is, of course, Jane Eyre, who can only return to Rochester when he is crippled and blind.

The "Gloria Victis" foreshadows the Hubers' relationship. Karl becomes blind after accidentally infecting his eye with a culture in his laboratory. His identity, his potency, as a research scientist is eradicated, and Ernestine must support and mother him.

> Her mothering instinct had been supreme that summer. It had dominated her so completely as to blur slightly the clearness of her intellectual vision. To be doing things for him, making him as comfortable as possible, to find occupation for him as one does for the convalescent, to hover about him, showering him with manifestations of her love and woman's protectiveness — it had stirred the mother in her, and in the depths of her sorrow there had been a sublime joy (189).

Glaspell's surface meaning is undoubtedly "the sublime joy" of self-sacrifice, but the phrase may also somewhat sinisterly signal Ernestine's ultimate chance for power or autonomy.

After some attempts to keep painting despite Karl's deepening depression, Ernestine uses Karl's illness as a chance to surrender the frightening challenge of her own career to the conventional excuse of her husband's needs. She decides to study scientific methods in Karl's old laboratory at the University in order to act as Karl's eyes.

> I shall strive to become a perfectly constructed instrument — that's all. And I *will* be better than the usual laboratory assistant, for not having any ideas of my own. I will not intrude my individuality upon Karl — to blur his vision (205–206).

To perform this miracle of selflessness, she needs to denigrate her own art: "Karl's work is the more important. Nobody is going to die for a water colour or an oil painting" (206).

Ernestine continues to relinquish art in favor of science until she attends an exhibition by a noted Norwegian artist. From the novel's descriptions of his paintings, this artist is probably based on Fritz Thaulow, who exhibited his work at the Art Institute of Chicago from January 15 through 28, 1903, the year Glaspell was in Chicago. Like Ernestine, he is a landscapist whose paintings contain water in the forms of rivers, streams, and waterfalls. The catalogue of the exhibition raises other parallels since Thaulow's "father was a distinguished chemist, and his grandfather a painter," reminiscent of the split between Ernestine's scientific father and artistic mother. Thaulow is also described as a somewhat androgynous figure: "In person he is of imposing height and has all the typical appearance of the men of the North; he combines with an equable temper full of charm, a most sympathetic nature."[17]

When Ernestine stands before the Norwegian artist's work, she can no longer force herself to believe the relative insignificance of art for humanity's future because the paintings suggest that the artist is the mother of the best in humanity. "They drew her to them as the mother the homesick child. . . . a home-coming of the spirit — the heart's passionate thankfulness, the heart's response" (271). Ernestine is still unwilling to release these powers in herself; instead she decides that she must compromise and make her life a work of art so that "perhaps when the end of the world was reached, and all things translated in terms of universal things, to have done that would itself mean the painting of a masterpiece" (276).

Even this tentative aspiration is snatched from Ernestine when Karl dies. At his deathbed, she clings to him, "and, then, the strongest word of woman to man — 'I'm frightened! Oh take care of

me — Karl — take care of me!'" (331). She regresses even further by
returning to her childhood home where she begins her penance of
futile domesticity, as if she believes her earlier hubris, her artistic
aspirations, had somehow killed Karl. She tells a visitor:

> I am making patchwork quilts! Can you find anything more
> worthless in this world than a patchwork quilt? — cutting things
> up and then sewing them together again, and making them uglier
> in the end than they were in the beginning? Do you know any-
> thing more futile to do with life than that? My aunt had begun
> some, and I am finishing them up (341).

Ernestine is certainly participating in what Myra Jehlen has described as a female "sub-culture born out of oppression and either
stunted or victorious only at often-fatal cost."[18]

These scenes indicate the terrifying conflict Glaspell sees between
a woman's gendered identity and art. While the narrative voice
seems to validate conventional pieties, positing that "the strongest
word of woman to man" is "take care of me," Ernestine's utter
misery and her bitter comments about the domestic art relegated to
women belie nineteenth-century platitudes. Glaspell needed to find
a way for Ernestine to have her cake and eat it too, to appear to
fulfill her gender role and her potential as an artist. She does so by
having Ernestine paint her own "Gloria Victis," a portrait of Karl
at the moment of his death when he realizes how much she loved
him.

The painting is a tremendous success, "a masterpiece of light"
(373), but Glaspell does not allow Ernestine to take credit for the
triumph.[19] Ernestine has won through her maternal feelings: "Karl
asked for a child of their love. And at the last it was the call of the
child to the mother which she heard. It was the maternal instinct
of the spirit which answered. . . . she saw the picture which she
would paint" (364). The last words of the novel are a question
Ernestine asks Karl's spirit, "Did I indeed bring you the light?"
(376), as if her accomplishment does not exist without his validation. Although Ernestine sees a greater, less personal purpose in
her work, that too is inextricably linked with Karl, "to show how
she and Karl loved the world, what they held it worth" (375).

The Glory of the Conquered is a deeply conflicted novel, which
shows that Glaspell had yet to emerge completely from the plots

and values of her nineteenth-century literary mothers so well described by Nina Baym:

> The writers' conviction that character had to adjust to limiting circumstances, their belief that suffering and hardship could not be avoided in any human life, and their strenuous insistence that such trials, because they called out otherwise dormant abilities, could become occasions for "perfecting" the character imply a deeply Victorian world view.[20]

In *The Glory of the Conquered*, Glaspell seems largely to share this world view since Ernestine is only allowed an artistic triumph after great suffering, and with the further proviso that the work derives from and is for others, not herself. Karl presides in his portrait and in Ernestine's deference to his views, but he is conveniently out of the way of her actual accomplishment after she has paid her dues by serving him.

The Glory of the Conquered, however, is a transition novel that points to modernity in that Ernestine does achieve a nondomestic career and she does see herself as an artist with a calling or vocation, not simply someone writing professionally to pay for home and hearth. At this point in her career, Glaspell did not recognize the social and systemic causes of Ernestine's plight, but upheld the nineteenth-century view that the individual of strong character could triumph over her personal problems; in other words, *The Glory of the Conquered* is the turn-of-the-century version of the Myth of the Superwoman, who "has it all," though sequentially rather than simultaneously.

3

"Fidelity"
to the Future through
"Visioning"

Glaspell's second novel, *The Visioning* (1911), is a marked departure from the somewhat tradition-bound *The Glory of the Conquered* (1909). If Glaspell tentatively questions the cult of domesticity in her first novel, in her second she vigorously challenges society in its many aspects: religion, war, the class structure, capitalism, inherited wealth, tradition, and the double standard of gender roles. *The Visioning* shocked reviewers, friends, and family who had greatly enjoyed her more conventional novice effort.[1] As if to ask her religious, respectable mother for understanding, Glaspell dedicated *The Visioning* to her. Glaspell and *The Visioning*'s heroine, like many turn-of-the-century American women writers, confronted what Elizabeth Ammons describes as "the need to find union and reunion with the world of one's mother, particularly as one journeyed farther and farther from that world into territory traditionally marked off as forbidden."[2]

The catalyst for Glaspell's change was, of course, her relationship with George Cram Cook, the married Thoreauvian truck farmer, and her participation in Davenport's Monist Club, comprised of socialists as well as idealistic seekers of various ilks. At first, Glaspell's interest in socialism seemed frivolous, a game to be played with Cook for the pleasure of collaborating with him on a novel. In an undated letter, probably written in 1910, Cook relates this anecdote to his friend and fellow writer Floyd Dell:

> Susan and I had a day of creative energy here about a girl going
> to the city to seek her social salvation—a *questess*—you will rec-
> ognize the model. We telephoned the model to come down and
> tell the story of her life—we wanted to put her in a book. She
> did—and somehow the reality—graver, weightier than our incipi-
> ent dream, overwhelmed us. Before that, Susan wanted to play
> with a socialist-individualist contrast between the girl and the
> man, and I suggested having them each convert the other and
> wind up on the other side. We rejoiced in that until our model
> arrived and then—her socialism is such a deep slow growth hav-
> ing so many roots far back in her experience that we felt how
> shallow and unreal it was to try to uproot such a thing.[3]

Although her collaboration with Cook did not materialize, "the
model's" visit evidently made a deep impression on Glaspell, for
the conversion of *The Visioning*'s heroine to socialism is sparked
by her unanticipated intimacy with a woman from another class,
in addition to her mentoring by an iconoclastic male socialist.

At the beginning of *The Visioning*, Katherine Wayneworth Jones
seems to be made in the image of the American Girl as cultural
icon. Unlike the stationary, plump, silent madonna revered by the
nineteenth-century, Katie is rather androgynous: slender, lively,
witty, and athletic; she plays golf and even pilots her own boat.
Her suitor, the conventional Captain Prescott, wonders "why a girl
who had so many of the attributes of a boy should be so much
more fascinating than any mere girl."[4] Since she lives on an army
base with her officer brother, surrounded by military friends and
admirers, she seems a living embodiment of a contemporary ideal.
Martha Banta writes, "once the [American] Girl became the symbol
for the nation as a political entity, she was assigned as a strong
image harboring explicitly imperialistic connotations."[5] As befits a
cherished icon, Katie leads a sheltered life: the army post is located
on an island and functions as an ordered, secure world unto itself.

As a venturesome American Girl, not a statue or image, Katie
has difficulty finding role models. The lives of the staid Army
wives are characterized by "the dreariness and desolation of pleasure" (3). Katie's prospective mother-in-law epitomizes decorum:
"Mrs. Prescott did not, in any form, say things were as they were;
it was only that she breathed it" (204). Clara, the ex-wife of Katie's
brother Wayne, has left army life for Paris, but she was motivated

by hedonism, not a spirit of protest. The young women from out-side the base who are considered fit associates for Katie are repre-sented by a wealthy manufacturer's daughter, Caroline Osborne, whose idea of helping the less fortunate is giving a garden party for the girls who work in her father's factory for fifty cents an hour (161). Katie seems to believe that the women she knows lead such futile lives because it is peacetime. Although she is naive about what constitutes privation, she admires and envies her dead mother's more adventurous life at frontier army posts, "going to outlandish spots of the earth, braving danger and doing without cooks!" (382).

Katie's ennui ends when she prevents a young lower-class chorus girl from drowning herself on the island. She takes the young woman, who calls herself Verna Woods, home with her, renames her the classier Ann Forrest, and decides to remake her in the image of army ladies in order to introduce her into society as a visiting friend. As is typical of Glaspell's heroines, she believes that she is befriending Ann out of maternal feeling since Ann seems "like a child that has had a cruel time and needs to be comforted" (18). In actuality, Katie wants to use Ann as a sort of alter ego to supply vicariously the worldly knowledge her own privileged status obviates. She tells Ann, "Your education has been one-sided. So has mine. Perhaps we can strike a balance" (59).

Katie finds another source of information in a boat repairman and aspiring playwright, Alan Mann, a representative socialist of that time and place. He is a skilled craftsman, not an unskilled laborer, as was typical of the non-urban socialism of the Midwest.[6] Like George Cram Cook, he is not a hard-core Marxist, but a democratic idealist who lends Katie books on evolution, socialism, and working women. Katie is attracted by his strength, physical and ideological, yet his caste and manner prevent him from seem-ing threatening to her.

> His sleeves were rolled up; he had no hat, no coat. He had been working with something muddy. A young man, a large man, and strong. The first thing which she saw as distinctive was the way his smile lived on his lips, as if his thought was smiling at the smile (172).

In fact, he looks like one of Glaspell's favorite poets, Walt Whit-man, in the frontispiece to that great work of democratic idealism, *Leaves of Grass.*

The course of this female *bildungsroman* seems clear in a passage about Ann and Katie's developing relationship:

> They were that most intimate of all things in the world, two girls with a secret, two girls set apart from all the world by that secret they held from all the world, hugging between them a beautiful, brilliant secret and laughing at the rest of the world because it couldn't get in (88).

In a pattern typical of Glaspell's fiction, she is setting up her heroine and her reader for a fall because this cozy picture of sisterhood could as easily be attributed to Katie's naive point of view as to Glaspell's omniscient narrator. Katie is really playing with Ann, as a little girl does with her doll, or as a novelist does with her characters: "From out the nothing a conscious something I have evoked. It would be most ungracious — ungrateful — of Ann to refuse to be what I made her. I invented her" (35).

A little girl and her doll or a novelist with her characters are two relatively benign characterizations of Katie's attitude toward Ann, but two other patterns of imagery depicting this attitude are more problematic. In the first pattern, Ann is metaphorically linked to dogs. Katie associates Ann with a cringing cur whom Katie helps but who is eventually killed by a servant on the Army base.[7] Ann is judged by the way she relates to Katie's nephew's dogs, and Katie defends the character of her uncle the Bishop by citing his love for his dog. Ann's blighted background is brought home to Katie when she learns that Ann had to kill her pet dog because her sadistic father wanted to take it away from Ann to a place where it could not be happy. Ann comments, "I could have stood my own lonesomeness. But what I couldn't stand was thinking about him. . . . I couldn't keep from thinking things that tortured me" (285). This, of course, is also Katie's developing attitude toward girls like Ann. In the next paragraph, in a subconscious association of Ann and her dog, Katie thinks, "She had loved Ann because Ann needed her, been tender to her because Ann was her charge" (286).

Glaspell loved dogs and her fiction abounds with portraits of devotion between owner and dog, but this is not an equal relationship; the owner does the thinking and gives the orders, and the dog obeys and is grateful. In a sense, this is a paradigm of bad mothering in that the mother does the thinking instead of encouraging the child to think for herself. Katie cannot yet move beyond noblesse oblige or smothering maternity in her relationship with Ann.

Although the relationship between owner and dog does have a certain nobility, the relationship between owner and weapon is more sinister. Katie at first compares Ann to a "bullet" (5) that has been "just shot into my life" (58), and attempts to overcome her feelings of confusion and vulnerability by seizing a weapon herself. When she compares herself unfavorably to her brother Wayne, an inventor of weapons, she muses:

> "It is the gun. . . . Had the same ancestors myself, and yet I'm both less and more of them than he is. What I need's a gun! Then I'd stand out of the background better, too." . . . Ann! Might not Ann be her gun? . . . Perhaps every one felt the gun need to make them less the product and more the person (78–79).

Though *The Visioning* antedates Glaspell's life in intensely Freudian Greenwich Village, this sounds like a clear case of penis envy, but in the context of the novel, it is clear that Katie wants to control someone in the way the patriarchy, symbolized by her brother and the army, controls women. Katie wants power, but she does not yet know that there is a more desirable power that is wielded with others, not gained at their expense.

As the dog and gun imagery suggest, Katie is using Ann to make herself feel needed and powerful. Her friendship cannot stand the test of two revelations about Ann's past. Ann tells her that she stole the money that she needed to escape from her cruel father and go to the city. Later she informs her that as an exploited urban working girl, she surrendered to a seducer in the guise of a protector; he was Major Darrow, another of Katie's current suitors. Katie's revulsion at these "crimes" precipitates Ann's departure for parts unknown. Privileged Katie cannot conceive of the need to escape harsh reality through the promise of love and security, however illusory, that Ann calls her "Something Somewhere" (234).

Through Katie's search for Ann in the city, Glaspell paints a portrait of what Joanne Meyerowitz calls the "woman adrift," a single working woman in Chicago at that time.[8] In one key incident during her search for Ann through the working woman's wasteland, Katie sees for herself the telephone office where Ann worked and realizes that it "seemed a mammoth nervous system, feeding on other nervous systems, lesser sacrificed to greater" (297), a vision of Darwinian horror, the survival of the fittest. Katie can now see how Ann lost her health and her nerves, leaving her ripe for Major Darrow's plucking.

Glaspell's depiction of Ann's "fall" fits two contemporary paradigms. In novels of the 1880s and 1890s about women adrift, Meyerowitz finds that "this literature presented a caricature of the woman adrift as helpless victim," the volitionless Victorian virgin becoming volitionless Victorian whore.[9] Glaspell is also reflecting the contemporary socialist line on women and prostitution as expressed, for example, by Philip Rappaport in 1906: "The prostitute is the helpless victim of modern economic conditions, not industry alone. Among the hundreds of thousands of saleswomen and typewriters there are comparatively few who receive a compensation sufficient for their support."[10]

In either case, and in Glaspell's case, the lower-class woman is presented as helpless; she must be saved by a knight in shining armor or the rise of the proletariat. Ann is rescued by her knight, Katie's brother Wayne, who has joined the forest service as penance for his complicity with the military-industrial complex; he will take Ann with him as his wife. Wayne can transcend his class and gender prejudices because of his maternal feeling toward Ann, which he discovers when she is ill and alone: "Then he would make her care for him by caring for her — caring for her protectingly, tenderly, surrounding her with that sea of tenderness that was in his heart for her" (377). The ennoblement of maternal feeling is also available to, but rarely displayed by, Glaspell's male characters, but the problem here is that Wayne is allowed to rise morally while Ann must stay enclosed in the womb, "that sea of tenderness." Glaspell depicts her as so traumatized by her experiences that she retreats to the cult of domesticity as Wayne's wife. "Ann had found joy and peace — safety — and was too happy in her own life to get excited about the world" (447).

Glaspell's version of the New Woman is not the working-class woman of the Old World, comprised of eastern and midwestern small towns and cities, but a woman from a New World, the American west. Wayne and Katie's cousin Fred had earlier defied his father the bishop, joined the forest service, and become engaged to Helen, a clerk in the forest service. Helen believes that women should work, even after marriage. She has "some kind of theory about the economic independence of woman" (133), states Fred, who also remarks that "manly authority doesn't faze Helen much" (133). He then tellingly remarks to Katie, "She's very much what you would have been if you'd lived out there and had the advantages she has" (134). Neither Katie nor Ann can achieve a similarly feminist stance because of their molding in the caste-and-gender-ridden Old World.

Unlike Helen, Katie is only capable of marrying her mentor, not her equal, and only after various incidents provoke further anguished challenges to her life and values, one of which Glaspell uses to lead to the happy ending. Katie learns that one reason Alan Mann so hates the military is his court-martial for striking an officer in defense of an enlisted man. After all Katie has seen and learned, it seems hardly credible that this would upset her to the point of spurning him, but it does, and she broods over her ancestral military tradition. In a not very convincing conversation, Katie first sees herself as a "pathetically festive little monkey; and society was the clown holding the string—the whole of it advertising the tawdry thing the clown called life" (451). She then sees a contrasting version of life in a gardener, who "was wise and tender in taking the old things away, that the new shoots might have air" (452–53). Katie emulates the gardener's nurturing acts and casts off her "old things," her inherited conventions so that at the end of the novel she is reunited with Alan Mann. They form the perfect socialist couple, for, in the novel's final words, "in their two hearts there seemed love enough to redeem the world" (464).

Katie's romance with Alan Mann seems contrived; it is much less compelling and much less developed than the story of Katie's relationship with Ann. Perhaps Glaspell was simply fantasizing about what she hoped to achieve with the still married Cook, but she also may have been trying to portray the ideal heterosexual relationship for socialists of her generation, as described by Mari Jo Buhle in *Women and Socialism*: "The uniquely close association between men and women set the new intellectuals apart from most elder Socialists, not merely because their private lives were so intense but because even their political organizations bore the impact of heterosexuality."[11]

Katie and Alan may be similarly together, but not exactly as one since in the novel's conclusion, Katie sweetens Alan's rational socialism by showing him the power of love, reflecting the nine-teenth-century stereotypes of men as thinkers and women as emot-ers. Deborah Silverton Rosenfelt notes that "the conflation of ro-mantic love and social passion in such passages reflects a certain confusion about both desire and politics characteristic of the era and the milieu."[12] Glaspell may also be trying to make socialism palatable to herself and her readers by combining it with her ro-mantic belief in the power of love, an idea scorned by contempo-rary socialists such as Charles H. Kerr, who wrote in 1906, "The sentimental Utopian says that people will come to realize how beau-tiful and heavenly it would be to live together in love, and that therefore he hopes to see the capitalist resign their privileges and help establish a new republic based on human brotherhood. But this is not the answer of a Socialist."[13]

The real problem with *The Visioning*, though, is that Glaspell is groping toward her true subject, the plight of women and the ways they overcome it, but her ostensible subject, perhaps under Cook's influence, is a laundry list of social problems that will somehow be eradicated by socialism. Glaspell's imagination was never funda-mentally engaged by political theories, but her examination of women's lives in *The Visioning* helped prepare her for feminism as she would experience it in Greenwich Village's Heterodoxy Club after her marriage to Cook in 1913. What she learned in the Vil-lage, and in her marriage, would make her next novel, *Fidelity* (1915), quite different from *The Visioning* in subject and treat-ment.

Many socialists hoped for the equality of the sexes, but they believed it would occur as part of a new world-order; it was not a goal to be pursued immediately and independently. As Mari Jo Buhle states,

> Feminists had a different perspective on social change. They downplayed the collective advancement of women into civil soci-ety for the practice of personal development and the goal of self-realization. Feminists judged the socialist party not only in-adequate to respond to their needs but archaic in certain key respects.[14]

This quest for "self-realization" was the purpose of the Heterodoxy Club, a women's luncheon club founded in Greenwich Village in 1911, and it was promoted by the agreement that nothing said at the meetings would be conveyed to outsiders. As Dee Garrison writes,

> In many ways Heterodoxy functioned like the feminist conscious-
> ness-raising groups of the 1960s, enabling the women to know
> one another on intimate terms and to discover their mutual
> rage — a sympathetic female support group nowhere else available
> to its members.[15]

Susan Glaspell's membership in this group helped make *Fidelity* a novel about a woman, Ruth Holland, who gradually perceives that her individual plight is shared by other women; her conversations with an enlightened female contemporary give her the impetus to change her thinking and her situation. Appropriately, *Fidelity* is dedicated to Lucy Huffaker, Glaspell's college chum, who remained her close friend into and beyond her Greenwich Village days.

In contrast to Glaspell, Ruth Holland is not blessed with such a supportive female friend of her youth. Like *The Visioning*'s Katie, she is surrounded by conventional women. The older generation of ironically named Freeport resembles *The Visioning*'s decorum-worshipping Mrs. Prescott in their tribalism. Ruth's friend Deane Franklin muses, "how hard it was for women whose experiences had all fallen within the circle of things as they should be to understand a thing that was — disrupting. It was as if their kindly impulses, sympathy, tenderness, were circumscribed by that circle."[16] Ruth realizes that "she had never talked with her mother of real things, had never talked with her of the things of her deepest feelings" (116) because they would so clearly fall beyond the range of her cautiously circumscribed reality. A socially prominent younger matron, Marion Williams, presents only a "calm surface," that is "so poised, so cool" (54) as her defense and revenge against her unfaithful husband Stuart. Unlike Glaspell's Davenport, Freeport apparently has no Monist Club so Ruth is left to the society of young women like her best friend, the sweet but conventional Edith Blair, and a bolder-thinking but ineffectual male admirer, Deane Franklin.

Also like Katie, Ruth and Edith are so sheltered that they seem incapable of passing beyond girlhood. Years later, Ruth recognizes that "they were singularly unmatured for girls of twenty. . . . Life had dealt too favoringly and too uneventfully with them to find out what stuff was really in them" (38–39). Restive Ruth had tried to find herself by asking that she be sent away to college but was refused by her father who was afraid of education "unfeminizing" (40–41) her. Glaspell is not suggesting that higher education is a panacea for Ruth, or other young women, but that they need an outlet for their vitality and a direction in which to grow.

> With Ruth the desire to go to college had been less a definite craving for knowledge than a diffused longing for an enlarged experience. . . . Her energies having been shut off from the way they had wanted to go, she was all the more zestful for new things from life (41–42).

In Glaspell's works, the life force always seeks expression, even if it is forced to take an alternate channel that perverts it from its true potential, and so it is with Ruth whose *élan vital* becomes directed into the illicit excitement of a love affair with the conventional businessman-philanderer Stuart Williams, husband of the "cool" and "poised" Marion.

Although I have chronologically related Ruth's history to this point in order to point to some parallels with Katie Jones's youth, the novel actually begins *in medias res*, with Ruth's return to the bedside of her dying father eleven years after she has run away from Freeport with Stuart. Her mother had died earlier with Ruth's name on her lips. Some, like Dr. Deane Franklin, believe pneumonia was the cause of death while others, like Edith Lawrence's censorious mother, assert that she "died of a broken heart" (3) in the aftermath of Ruth's flight, a scandal her family could not seem to live down. Her older brother Cyrus is embittered and unforgiving, her sister Harriett seems to be repenting for Ruth's sins as the cowed wife of a peculiarly uncharitable Christian minister, and her younger brother Ted is a confused and rebellious young man. Like her prototype, Mrs. Kramer in Glaspell's short story "Contrary to Precedent" (1904), Marion Williams remains intent on vengeance and continues to refuse to give Stuart a divorce. "Outraged pride blocked every path out from self. She was shut in with her power to inflict pain. That was all she had" (360).

Upon her return to Freeport, Ruth readily recognizes that the price of nonconformity is often more cruelly exacted upon the rebel's relations than the renegade herself; she is stricken "dumb in this new realization of how terrible it had been for them all" (197). Despite this heartrending portrayal of broken lives, through her depiction of Freeport's young matrons, the women Ruth could have become, Glaspell implies that Ruth really had no viable alternative to her escape. When Ruth is mentioned in conversation, her erstwhile best friend Edith, now Mrs. Blair, is "leaning to the far side of her big chair in order to escape the shaft of light from the porch lamp" (2). Ruth had recognized Edith's inability to confront reality eleven years earlier when Ruth could not bring herself to tell the betrothed Edith of her plans to run off with Stuart because she had "a confused sense of Edith as barricaded by her trousseau" (110).

Plainly, neither Ruth nor Glaspell advocates such a frightened retreat from life, but the more aggressive stance of Deane Franklin's new wife Amy, in the role Ruth could have played, is hardly any better. Amy is fast becoming another Marion Williams, a staunch defender of convention who is destroying her marriage through her suspicions about Deane's feelings for Ruth and her display of narrow-mindedness. Like Mrs. Kramer and Mrs. Williams, "she finally found control in that thought of her power over him used to make him suffer" (224). While Edith represents women who are afraid of power, Amy represents women who want power but only believe they have it if they can use it to best and hurt others in the subservient's desire to emulate the powerful, in this instance, men, very much as Katie had wanted to use Ann as her gun in *The Visioning*.

Although Ruth resembles neither Edith nor Amy, she is hardly unscathed by the experience of the past eleven years. Unlike Christine Holt in "Contrary to Precedent" or Ernestine Hubers in *The Glory of the Conquered*, Ruth is not an artist and appears to have no particular talents or inclinations toward a career. Unfortunately, maternity, Glaspell's alternate means of creativity for women, is also denied Ruth. A year before she left Freeport with Stuart, she had gone to Deane Franklin's office because "he was a doctor; he was her friend; she was in a girl's most desperate plight" (94). The text has no other indications of pregnancy so we are led to assume that he performed an abortion. Later, living with Stuart but unable to marry him, she is always "longing for a baby, [a] longing which circumstances made her sternly deny herself" (160).

In our first view of Ruth, as she returns on the train to Freeport, "when the baby [across the aisle] was crowing and laughing she abruptly turned away" (35).

Ruth is sad because of what her life lacks, not because she is a fallen woman. As Ann Ardis demonstrates in *New Women, New Novels: Feminism and Early Modernism*, "New Women novelists rethink the orthodox Victorian opposition between the 'pure' and the 'fallen' woman."[17] Similarly, Glaspell has moved beyond the stereotype of a helpless victim, such as *The Visioning*'s Ann Forrest, to a woman with a will who makes her own decisions, however difficult, and accepts their equally difficult consequences. Glaspell also shatters another romantic stereotype, that of the woman who considers the world well lost for love, in Ruth's realization that her relationship with Stuart has become deadening because "thoughts needed to be spoken. It opened something in one to speak them. With Stuart she had been careful not to talk of certain things, fearing to see him sink into that absorption, gloom, she had come to dread" (185).

When Ruth returns to Freeport, she is neither a penitent magdalene nor a happy romantic, but a woman who has no direction in life. Plainly, the women of Freeport society make a return to the fold neither possible nor desirable, but a woman who is an outsider, Annie Morris Herman, at least provides Ruth with a clue and acts as a catalyst. Annie had been a poor girl who always admired the socially prominent Ruth. Now she is a poor woman who must work hard on her farm to support her children and her "slow, stolid" (263) husband. She seems to have less than Ruth had or has, but she actually has more, and shares it with Ruth when she invites Ruth to visit her at the farm. Annie tells Ruth that "we keep alive by thinking" and that she has "made a world within" (265) by keeping her intellect alive. Like Cook and Glaspell's circle in Davenport, Annie has kept abreast of the exhilarating currents of change sweeping through the outside world, and she shares this knowledge with Ruth.

> A whole new world seemed to open from these things that were vital to Annie; there was promise in them — a quiet road out from the hard things of self. There were new poets in the world; there were bold new thinkers; there was an amazing new art; science was reinterpreting the world and workers and women were setting themselves free (269).

For Ruth, "it was like breaking out from a closed circle" (271).

In particular, Annie helps Ruth break away from her hackneyed notions about heterosexuality and maternity. Ruth feels that she has thrown away her life for love, but that love failed her. As had Glaspell in her maturing relationship with Cook, Annie has learned that "romantic love" is "the most beautiful thing in the world — while it lasts. . . . Sometimes it opens up to another sort of love — love of another quality — and to companionship. . . . With me, it didn't" (266). Annie was neither lost nor incomplete without romantic love, but held to her resolve "to be my *own!*" (267).

Annie similarly preserves herself from the nineteenth-century ideal of motherhood as self-immolation; she toils relentlessly for her children, but says, "in that working for them, I'm not going to let go of the fact that I count too" (273). Glaspell, through Ruth's responsive thoughts, redefines maternity.

> Thinking back to that it seemed to Ruth a bigger mother feeling than the old one. It was not the sort of maternal feeling to hem in the mother and oppress the children. It was love in freedom — love that did not hold in or try to hold in. It would develop a sense of the preciousness of life. It did not glorify self-sacrifice — that insidious foe to the fullness of living (273).

Through Annie, Glaspell is suggesting a kind of motherhood that begins with nurturing the mother herself; as a consequence, but not necessarily its *raison d'être*, the children have the benefit of a vital individual for a mother. This is motherhood as a challenge and challenging, not smothered and smothering.

Ruth's thoughts indicate that she has learned from Annie's views on love and maternity, but her actions demonstrate a regression. Like Ernestine Hubers in *The Glory of the Conquered* or Katie Jones in *The Visioning*, Ruth initially retreats from her exciting but risky new knowledge to what she perceives as safely conservative values. Mildred Woodbury, a young woman in love with a married man, seeks out Ruth, whom she idealizes, to affirm her decision to flaunt convention. In the light of her stultified relationship with Stuart and the warped lives of her family, Ruth is unfaithful to her belief in love and advises Mildred to take a trip to Europe with a local society matron. Mildred is sorely disillusioned but takes Ruth's advice, and her last appearance in the novel shows how she has profited from it: upon her return from Europe she is putting on airs about redecorating the family house and marrying a rich man. Ruth has failed Mildred as a spiritual mother; she has smothered her in security instead of challenging her to grow by taking a risk. As Mildred's surname suggests, Ruth has helped "bury" her in the fences, the "wood," of convention.[18]

Ruth also retreats by returning to Stuart. The harsh, cold life on their mountain sheep farm parallels the state of their relationship.

> Life had reduced itself to necessities; things had to be ruthlessly rearranged for meeting conditions. She loved her own room to sleep in. She needed it. But she had given that up because it was too cold, because she could not do any more work. There was something that made her cringe in the thought of their sharing a bed, not because of love of being together, but because of the necessity of fighting the cold (382).

Ruth has lost herself; her identity has been "*ruth*lessly rearranged" to suit a relationship as limited and boring as any conventional union. Once she realizes that she needs what Virginia Woolf calls "a room of one's own," she has the sense to reject Stuart's proposal of marriage which he makes, he tells her, "because we can now. Because it's the thing to do. Because it will be expected of us" (401). The possibility of an eternal union with this kind of thinker finally forces Ruth to confront the truth and end the relationship. As she later explains to her younger brother Ted, she now has a larger definition for the word "fidelity": "It isn't unfaithful to turn from a person you have nothing more to offer, for whom you no longer make life a living thing. It's more faithful to go" (419).

Ruth's epiphany has been made possible by Stuart's wife Marion who has experienced a similar self-discovery and decided to end her revenge and grant Stuart a divorce. Like Mrs. Kramer in "Contrary to Precedent," Marion has been changed by a vision of maternity. Ruth's brother Ted had shaken her complacency by visiting her unannounced and making an impassioned plea for Ruth. After lengthy self-scrutiny, she manifests her change of heart when she decides to retain, not fire, her maid Lily who is ill from a bungled abortion; she even declares that she will nurse the young woman herself when her righteous housekeeper refuses to have anything to do with Lily. She decides to consent to a divorce after realizing that "she wanted something from life. She must have more of that gentle sweetness that warmed her heart when Lily murmured, 'You're so kind!'" (376).[19]

Marion Williams chooses a tangible form of maternity in her nursing and championing of Lily, but Ruth Holland chooses to nurture both herself and humanity when at the end of the novel she decides to leave for New York because she believes "the war is going to make a new world — a whole new way of looking at things" (418). In *The Glory of the Conquered* and *The Visioning*, romantic love was depicted as the *sine qua non* of a woman's life, but in the last lines of *Fidelity*, Glaspell indicates that it is not an end in itself.

> Now she knew that love had not failed because love had tran-
> spired into life. What she had paid the great price for was not
> hers to the end. But what it had made of her was hers! Love
> could not fail if it left one richer than it had found one. Love
> had not failed — nothing had failed — and life was wonderful, lim-
> itless, a great adventure for which one must have great courage,
> glad faith. Let come what could come! — she was moving on
> (422).

Glaspell now defines romantic love as an important and enriching stage in a woman's life but it is just a stage; the continuous development of a woman's character and identity is what truly matters since as she nurtures herself, she nurtures humanity's future.

Carolyn Heilbrun comments on the patterns that women expect their lives to follow:

> We women have lived too much with closure: 'If he notices me,
> if I marry him, if I get into college, if I get this work accepted, if
> I get that job' — there always seems to loom the possibility of
> something being over, settled, sweeping clear the way for content-
> ment. This is the delusion of a passive life. When the hope for
> closure is abandoned, when there is an end to fantasy, adventure
> for women will begin.[20]

As the last words of *Fidelity* indicate, Ruth Holland resists closure and seeks adventure: "she was moving on." This phrase epitomizes Glaspell's belief in fidelity to the process, the "visioning," not the destination or conclusion. She continues to tell the stories of women "moving on" in her next works, somewhat conventionally in her novels, but quite radically in her plays.

4

Passive Resistance to Active Rebellion: From *Trifles* to *The Verge*

Glaspell did not publish a novel between *Fidelity* in 1915 and *Brook Evans* in 1928, the years of her involvement with the Provincetown Players, her sojourn in Greece with Cook, and her period of mourning for his death. She is, of course, best known for the plays she wrote during that period, particularly the widely anthologized *Trifles* (1916), and many critics consider the plays her major works because they are an exciting, innovative contribution to American drama. In terms of her fiction, though, the plays are not a startling flowering or reversal, but can be seen as the thematic and symbolic bridge between Glaspell's early and late novels.[1] In keeping with this thematic continuum, this chapter will examine the plays that focus on women, particularly the theme of maternity, for in these plays motherhood becomes disassociated from sweetness and light and increasingly linked to entrapment and oppression.[2] In contrast to the self-sacrificial struggles of Ernestine Hubers in *The Glory of the Conquered* (1909) or the long self-immolation of Ruth Holland in *Fidelity*, Glaspell creates dramatic heroines who begin to realize that in living for others they are destroying themselves. As Adrienne Rich states in her book on motherhood, "Oppression is not the mother of virtue; oppression can warp, undermine, turn us into haters of ourselves."[3]

Glaspell's fiction has been considered much more conventional than her plays, but the difference is one of degree; it is not a *volte face.* Although the heroines of her plays are more visibly, vocally, and sometimes violently, rebellious than those of her novels, her fictional heroines are hardly models of decorum. In *The Glory of the Conquered*, Ernestine Hubers manages to pursue her career as an artist and learn the methods of scientific research despite sexism on all sides; in *The Visioning*, Katie Jones leaves the safety and comfort of the military brass for the uncertainties of life with a socialist organizer and artist; although *Fidelity*'s Ruth Holland lives with a married man for years, she leaves him to pursue her own interests when he is free to marry but she no longer loves him.

Similarly, in formal terms, Glaspell's plays have been found more innovative than her fiction. For instance, the distinguished Eugene O'Neill and Glaspell scholar Linda Ben-Zvi states:

> Nothing in a Glaspell play is linear. Plots do not have clearly defined beginnings, middles, and ends; they self-consciously move out from some familiar pattern, calling attention as they go to the fact that the expected convention will be violated, the anticipated order will be sundered.[4]

Ben-Zvi is undoubtedly correct, but I see this difference as less a rebellion against the conventional well-made play and more of a continuation of some of the techniques of Glaspell's novels, which often begin *in medias res*, do not follow a conventional courtship to marriage pattern, and often end with the question of the heroine's future left open. Glaspell's dramatic use of understated gestures and comments also derives from her apprentice fiction; as early as 1904, her fictive heroine Christine Holt observes:

> At crucial times people acted just as they did in the commonplace hours—really they acted more so. And that would be a good feature to bring out in the play. The tragedy of the play must be very quiet, very conventional, and commonplace.[5]

The relative lack of action and plethora of ideas and meditative speeches in Glaspell's plays also arises from her work as a writer of women's fiction; in the restricted sphere of the domestic, a woman's life is mainly interior, inside her own mind as well as inside her home.

Glaspell's plays may not be formally or thematically antithetical to her fiction, but the difference in the degree of rebellion is significant. The rebellions of her fictional women are private while those of her dramatic heroines sometimes lead them to the public sphere of demonstrations, courts, and prison; these heroines do include two murderesses, a number of confessed adulteresses, and a police-basher. Their actions demand that the patriarchal world consider their feelings and situations as something more than domestic "trifles."

The increased degree of rebelliousness in Glaspell's plays has a number of causes, personal, generic, and cultural. First, in biographical terms, Glaspell was married to a believer and practitioner of free love whom she loved; she did not want to live without him, but his numerous affairs made him hard to live with, and her anger finds an outlet in these plays, sometimes quite specifically against Cook and sometimes against patriarchal men in general.[6] Secondly, her situation with the Provincetown Players as playwright, actress, and co-founder gave Glaspell an artistic freedom and control quite unusual for a woman. In *Feminist Theories for Dramatic Criticism*, Gayle Austin points out:

> The writing of plays requires mastering to some degree a male-dominated, public production machinery, something that relatively few women have been able to do over the long history of the form, and consequently there is not as large a body of extant plays by women as there is of novels.[7]

The liberating effect of Glaspell's transition to a different genre was augmented by her sense of a new audience: she was no longer trying to appeal to conventional middle-class female readers of fiction, but to the avant-garde of Greenwich Village and Provincetown, including her fellow members of the feminist Heterodoxy Club.

Glaspell's first solo dramatic effort is the justly celebrated one-act play *Trifles* (1916). Mrs. Peters and Mrs. Hale accompany some male authorities to the remote farmhouse of Minnie and John Wright where they are supposed to collect some personal belongings for the imprisoned Minnie while the men try to establish a motive for Minnie's alleged strangling of her husband. As numerous critics have demonstrated, the men stomp about loudly and authoritatively but cannot find the clues because they are unable to read quiet, domestic "trifles."[8] In contrast, Mrs. Peters and Mrs.

Hale realize that the disordered kitchen, ragged sewing, and stran-
gled canary indicate that the isolated Minnie would accept no further abuse from her cold, stingy husband and revenged the death
of her pet and friend by killing John the same way.[9] The women
display female solidarity by concealing the dead bird, and their
conclusions, from the men.

The sympathy of Mrs. Hale and Mrs. Peters arises not only
from sisterly solidarity but from the two women's self-identifica-
tion as mothers, in contrast to the childless Minnie. Love, particularly maternal love, is associated with sound and its absence with
silence. Mrs. Hale wonders "how it would seem never to have had
any children around," and Mrs. Peters can tell her: "I know what
stillness is. When we homesteaded in Dakota, and my first baby
died. . . ."[10] They realize that the pet was a kind of child-substitute
for the solitary Minnie; the canary's voice was to displace the silence
of a coldly authoritarian husband and replace the sounds of the unborn children. Mrs. Hale notes, "If there'd been years and years of
nothing, then a bird to sing to you, it would be awful—still, after the
bird was still" (26). Mrs. Peters even remembers a similar loss and
response: "When I was a girl—my kitten—there was a boy took a
hatchet, and before my eyes—and before I could get there—If they
hadn't held me back I would have—hurt him" (25).

Their maternal feelings not only help Mrs. Hale and Mrs. Peters
understand the importance of the canary to Minnie, but also help
them direct their solicitude toward Mrs. Wright herself through
the memory of Minnie as a vulnerable, pretty young girl who loved
singing in the choir. Mrs. Hale makes the identification clear when
she states that Minnie "was kind of like a bird herself—real sweet
and pretty, but kind of timid and—fluttery. How—she—did—
change" (22). Mrs. Hale finally places the blame for that change
on John Wright: "She used to sing. He killed that, too" (25).
Through the traditional literary metaphor of the bird's song as the
voice of the soul, the women acknowledge that John Wright not
only killed Minnie's canary, but her very spirit.

Adrienne Rich justly observes that "powerless women have always used mothering as a channel—narrow but deep—for their
own human will to power."[11] Similarly, Glaspell is not idealizing
motherhood or maternal feelings here but demonstrating that these
rural women have no outlets for expression aside from domes-

ticity focusing on children, though Minnie Wright lacks even that. After noting John Wright's nullity as a husband, Sharon P. Friedman states, "If a husband and children are the determinants of most women's lives, then Minnie has nothing; she is nothing."[12] Glaspell's early fiction repeatedly identifies artistic creativity with motherhood, but Minnie Wright is not allowed that outlet either, through an unfinished quilt or vicariously through the voice of the canary. In a sense, as Annette Kolodny has written, Glaspell is also exploring the plight of the woman writer; her "trifles" are as unnoticed and unappreciated by her culture as are Minnie's domestic artifacts by the investigating men.[13]

Glaspell demonstrates that maternal feelings are a double-edged sword in that they make Mrs. Hale and Mrs. Peters sympathize with Minnie's childlessness and want to protect her as if she were a child, but their maternal devotion also prevents them from helping Minnie until it is too late.[14] Mrs. Hale, played by Glaspell in the original production, declares, "I know how things can be — for women. We live close together and we live far apart. We all go through the same things — it's all just a different kind of the same thing" (27). She realizes that her narrow focus on her own domicile and children have kept her from nurturing Minnie, and cries, "Oh, I *wish* I'd come over here once in a while! That was a crime! That was a crime! Who's going to punish that?" (27). Not the men certainly, who want the women locked into separate domestic spheres and would like them to accept the blame, which really belongs to men. When she makes this comment Mrs. Hale is empathetic, but masochistic; not until she conceals the evidence with Mrs. Peters at the end of the play does she silently place the guilt where it really belongs.

If one regards Mrs. Hale and Mrs. Peters as the heroines of *Trifles*, their rebellion must be characterized not as active insurrection but as passive resistance, which is all these women can realistically achieve under the circumstances. If Minnie Wright is the central figure of *Trifles*, the play may seem different since she does murder her oppressor, but the glimpses we get of her after the killing, through Mr. Hale's spoken memories, indicate the ineffectual nature of her act. She has moved herself from her rocking chair in the center of the kitchen to a "small chair in the corner" (8), as if she is acknowledging her marginalized and outlaw status.

She keeps rocking as if she knows that she must comfort herself
the way a mother would a child. Most tellingly, she is largely silent,
except to laugh when Mr. Hale mentions that he came to see if
John Wright wanted a telephone and to tell him "I sleep sound" (7)
as her excuse for not hearing the killing. Both these sounds are in
effect silences that point to her past and future silencing: John had
cut her off from the sounds of human voices, and her sleep in the
grave will be sound and silent if she is convicted of murder. Even a
rebellious woman like Minnie knows that men may be laughable
in their blindness but that they still have overwhelming power.
Women like Mrs. Hale and Mrs. Peters are limited to the divisive
expression of biological maternity as a diversion from more culturally powerful creativity.

Glaspell's next play, *The People* (1917), does not ostensibly concern the position of women, but the character played by Glaspell
in the original production, the Woman from Idaho, is a spokesperson for the playwright, and her catalytic role indirectly comments
on the place of women in society.[15] A periodical based on *The
Masses, The People: A Journal of the Social Revolution*, is about
to fold because of insufficient funds and the competing idiosyncra-
sies of the staff. The real problem, though, is that the staff, most
importantly the Editor, have lost faith in the people and become
deracinated intellectuals.[16] They are recalled to their faith by three
representatives of the people who appear in the office: the Boy
from Georgia, who has left his date and a dance; the Man from
the Cape, who has left his oyster bed; and the Woman from Idaho,
who has left the tombstone she earned for herself as a form of
security.

The Woman from Idaho in many ways seems a continuation of
Fidelity's Ruth Holland who left the hinterlands for exciting new
cultural movements in New York City. The Woman describes her
vision from the train: she saw a plain with horses and cows the
way Ruth had perceived her western valley with sheep, a place of
confinement, conformity, silence, and death. It is also a landscape
that Minnie Wright would easily recognize.

A plain, dark trees off at the edge, against the trees a little house
and a big barn. A flat piece of land fenced in. Stubble, furrows.
Horses waiting to get in at the barn; cows standing around a

pump. A tile yard, a water tank, one straight street of a little town. The country so still it seems dead. The trees like—hopes that have been given up. The grave yards—on hills—they come so fast. I noticed them first because of my tombstone, but I got to thinking about the people—the people who spent their whole lives right near the places where they are now. There's something in the thought of them—like the cows standing around the pump. So still, so patient, it—kind of hurts. And their pleasures:—a flat field fenced in.[17]

Only the words of the Editor of *The People* had managed to bestir her from this landscape of pure physicality ending in death.

By the end of the play, however, the Woman from Idaho has herself become so articulate that she inspires the Editor and his staff to continue to publish their journal; in other words, she seems like an embodiment of the traditional woman as the muse of an artistic man, but Glaspell manages to evade this trap: although the Woman from Idaho is meant to be a representative of the silent masses, she is actually much more eloquent than the intellectuals at the office, as her speech describing the rural deathscape indicates. In the context of the play, her change is caused because the words of the Editor fertilized her so that she brought forth inspirational speech: "When my work was done that night, I read your wonderful words. They're like a spring—if you've lived in a dry country, you'll know what I mean" (54). Like a pregnant woman, she is an icon of the past, the present, and the future, and her speech, like that of a child, spurs its father, the Editor, to work for the future in the endless evolutionary progress that is Glaspell's vision of maternal creativity for men and women. Only the Woman from Idaho realizes that the social revolution is not a product, but a process: "*Seeing*—that's the Social Revolution" (57), Glaspell's Greenwich-Village version of *The Visioning*.

In *The People*, Glaspell presents men and women alternately inspiring one another in an endless creative process, but in *The Outside* (1917) she initially depicts women without men, and they seem as sterile as the landscape that surrounds them. Mrs. Patrick has left her husband over some unspecified betrayal and is living in bitterness in an appropriately abandoned lifesaving station on Cape Cod with her silent servant Allie Mayo who lost her husband to the sea twenty years earlier.[18] The women's willed wasteland is invaded and revivified by two male life-savers who bring in a drowned man. Despite Mrs. Patrick's seemingly callous attempts to drive them out, they attempt to resuscitate him. Their efforts are unsuccessful, but the example of their fervor and persistence seems to bring Allie Mayo back to life, as the words of The Editor had revived The Woman from Idaho. Allie Mayo was played by Glaspell in the original production, and like Mrs. Hale and the Woman from Idaho, is her spokesperson. She tells Mrs. Patrick, "For twenty years, I did what you are doing. And I can tell you—it's not the way."[19]

The women's situation is examined through the title image, "the outside." They live outside the town where the last vegetation meets the sand "on the outside shore of Cape Cod" (99). The life-savers see the vegetation as valiant, as courageous as their own efforts to save the drowning man, but like that effort, they believe it is opposed by Mrs. Patrick. Bradford declares, "I believe she *likes* to see the sand slippin' down on the woods. Pleases her to see somethin' gettin' buried, I guess" (105). The vegetation is ugly, stunted by its struggle against wind and sand, but Allie Mayo tells Mrs. Patrick that it should be valued because "strange little things that reach out farthest" are the necessary beginnings of life "and hold the sand for things behind them. They save a wood that guards a town" (112) where "children live" (113).

As Linda Ben-Zvi has observed, "The image of pioneering is a recurrent one in all of Glaspell's plays; it shapes all her writing."[20] Pioneering is also closely associated with motherhood for Glaspell, as in the image of the vegetation on the outside sheltering the children within. Mrs. Patrick seems to realize this in her last speech of the play, "Meeting the Outside!", which she "cannot say . . . mockingly . . . ; in saying it, something of what it means has broken through, rises. Herself lost, feeling her way into the wonder of life" (117). The last line of the play, one which surely only the most gifted of actresses could convey, is the bracketed stage direction, "It grows in her as slowly (Curtain)" (117). The line is incomplete, but one possible conclusion is that "it grows in her as slowly as a child," that "wonder of life." To pioneer for humanity is a form of motherhood because it also prepares the way for the future, and in *The Outside* Glaspell depicts two women who may become such pioneers, though they are not biological mothers.

Glaspell's next play, *Woman's Honor* (1918), is her finest comedy because the humor and the message are mutually supportive, not detractive. In a sense, Glaspell's earlier plays had also addressed the question of a woman's honor. Is it more honorable to murder your husband than endure his abuse? Is women's honor better served by concealing a crime than revealing it to a male-dominated judiciary that cannot fathom its motive? Is honor maintained by the respectability of earning your own tombstone or by continuing to grow and live in raffish Greenwich Village? Do women without men, women on the outside, have any honor or importance at all? In *Woman's Honor* Glaspell hilariously explores competing definitions of that term while exploding the double standard.

Gordon Wallace, a prisoner, faces a death sentence because he refuses to provide an alibi for the night of October twenty-fifth; he declares himself "ready to die to shield a woman's honor."[21] In a conference room at the sheriff's house, his lawyer Mr. Foster tells him that he had determined to save him from his "romantic course" (122) by publishing the story in the newspaper so that "wives — including, I hope, jurors' wives — will cry, 'Don't let that chivalrous young man die!'" (123). Six women appear in the room, five of them ready to sacrifice their honor by claiming that they were with Wallace on the night in question. They are identified by their particular feminine roles, not individual names, as if to emphasize the ways the concept of woman's honor warps the lives of all sorts of women. Three embody positive cultural myths, such as the Virgin Madonna, and three epitomize the negative ones, such as witch-bitch.

The Silly One is the virgin, a foolish one at that, since she wants to give up her honor for the romantic notion of saving a knight, the equally silly Gordon Wallace. Her inability to perceive reality is demonstrated when she at first embraces Mr. Foster, mistaking him for Wallace. She speaks in romantic cliches, such as "Love is so beautiful. So ennobling!" (132) and "Love conquereth all things" (135). By the end of the play, through her exposure to the other women, she has shifted her allegiance further from romantic clap-trap and closer to feminist solidarity when she tells the Shielded One, "I will give my life for yours, my sister!" (148). Her consciousness may have changed its focus, but not necessarily been raised, since her last line in the play is "Love is so beautiful!" (155).

The Shielded One is maiden as prospective wife, a wealthy young woman whose honor will be preserved so that she will best exhibit the status of her husband. Her discomfort with her role as icon and commodity is displayed by her willingness to surrender her "honor," and by the questions she raises: "What *is* woman's honor?" (144); "Aren't we more than things to be noble about?" (145); and "Is it true that women will not help one another? That they are hard and self-seeking?" (151). As the latter question indicates, she wants sisterly solidarity, not the divisive competition over men that she views as a form of prostitution: "I speak for all the women of my . . . —under-world, all those others smothered under men's lofty sentiments toward them! I wish I could paint for you the horrors of the shielded life. [*Says 'shielded' as if it were 'shameful'.*]" (146). The parody of a fate worse than death continues as she declares of the shielded life, "I'd rather die than go back to it!" (147).

The Motherly One represents the Madonna, a woman beyond sexuality who consequently has no "honor" worth saving in a culture that values women as commodities for their appearance and ability to give sexual pleasure. She is a nurse who sees sacrificing her "honor" as an extension of her roles as mother and professional. She regards men as spoiled children who treat the concept of woman's honor like a toy. "I should really hate to take it from them entirely" (145), she indulgently observes, but she recognizes that the toy can be dangerous unless she places it under her maternal purview: "It would be just like a lot of men to fuss around about a woman's honor and really let it hurt somebody" (136). By the end of the play, the Motherly One becomes more interested in nurturing her fellow women than in preserving the inane Wallace; she tries to provide them with opportunities for speech and mediates their competing claims.

The Mercenary One is the ostensibly negative counterpart of the Silly One since she also does not understand what is happening, but for quite different reasons. She has come to the prison to apply for a stenographer's job. She needs to make a living and has no time for abstractions such as woman's honor. The other women mistakenly believe that she has arrived to sell Wallace her reputation so that he can save his life; they accuse her of being "hard" and lacking "woman's self-respect" (142). Glaspell is quite clearly indicating that the shelter and trap of woman's honor is restricted to a materially privileged group of women who are too caste-ridden to empathize with a woman who must work outside her home.

In effect, the women have accused the Mercenary One of a kind of prostitution, but, unlike the Shielded One, they do not recognize the kind of prostitution to which women subject themselves in the name of love. The Scornful One, however, does perceive it, as her name indicates. She was outside the privileged class of women whose honor is shielded so that one man alone may own it. To the assembled women, she describes the hypocrite who took her honor when she was seventeen: "Why, this instant his eyes would become 'pools of feeling' if any one were to talk about saving a woman's honor" (139). She is the most realistic of the women, the one who can truly understand that the concept of woman's honor is a way to limit and dehumanize women: "Woman's honor is only about one thing, and . . . man's honor is about everything but that thing" (134). Without the privilege, or burden, of a woman's honor, she is free to be the best person she can: "You see honor camouflages so many things — stupidity, selfishness — greed, lust, avarice, gluttony. So without it you're almost forced to be a decent sort — and that's sometimes wearing" (139).

The Scornful One's derision is directed not only at hypocritical men, but at her fellow women who have not been compelled to develop her kind of strength, particularly the "coward" (137) who was really with Wallace on October twenty-fifth but will not appear to save him. Although the Scornful One had initially wanted to destroy the concept of woman's honor through her parodic sacrifice, by the play's end she wants all the women to work together to preserve the young and salvageable, "to save *both* of them [the Shielded One and the Silly One] through Gordon Wallace" (155); in other words, she wants to make women the subjects here and a man their object or tool.

The sixth woman who appears is the Cheated One, played by Glaspell in the original production. She has lived the respectable monogamous life of the Motherly One, but there is no indication in the text that she has been relieved of her role as sex object through having children. She tells the other women,

> I've been cheated. Cheated out of my chance to have a man I
> wanted by a man who would have what he wanted. Then he

> saved my woman's honor. Married me and cheated me out of my
> life. I'm just something to be cheated. That's the way I think of
> myself. Until this morning. Until I read about Gordon Wallace.
> Then I saw a way to get away from myself. It's the first thing I
> ever wanted to do that I've done. You'll not cheat me out of this.
> Don't you try! (154)

The rape of her body followed by the matrimonial rape of her
spirit has made her as suspicious of her fellow women as she is of
men. She is so embittered that even her way of getting away from
herself is actually an affirmation of that self: "The only unfortu-
nate woman I'll think about is myself" (154). At the end of the
play, she is still unable to join the huddle of women, but she does
hover about the edge if only "not to be cheated of what is being
said" (156). Through the Cheated One, Glaspell is demonstrating
that a woman's martyrdom for honor does not make her a saint,
but quite the contrary: the repeated denial of a woman's identity
and volition can make her a monster of selfishness as she desperately tries to compensate herself for what has been wrested from
her.

Gordon Wallace claims to esteem women so highly that he would
die for their honor, but his misogynistic use of chivalry is un-
masked at the conclusion of the play. He is so horrified by the
sight of the united women that when a seventh woman appears,
"large and determined" (156), he declares, "Oh, *hell. I'll plead
guilty*" (156), and the curtain descends. Christine Dymkowski
notes, "Men placed on the edge . . . are excluded from a power to
which they subscribe—Wallace, put in this position, cannot reshape his world from a new perspective; he can only affirm the old
one."[22] Or, as Sharon P. Friedman puts it, "He would rather die
than relinquish his control of the situation."[23] Gordon Wallace may
also be unwittingly speaking the truth because he and his fellow
subscribers to the concept of woman's honor are guilty of the dis-
honoring of woman's autonomy.

In a sense, *Bernice* (1919), Glaspell's first three-act play, is another version of *Woman's Honor*, with Bernice as an unselfish
version of the Cheated One; her philandering husband, the shallow
writer Craig Norris, as a more sophistic Gordon Wallace; and the
other women characters representing alternate women's roles. As
Act One begins, Bernice has died, and her father and devoted

servant Abbie await the return of Craig, his conventional sister Laura Kirby, and Bernice's closest friend, social activist Margaret Pierce. Upon their arrival, the examination of Bernice's life and motives begins, obtusely by the men and perceptively by most of the women, much as in the case of *Trifles*' Minnie Wright. Abbie later informs Craig that Bernice committed suicide, and Craig then takes "credit" by telling Margaret, "You think I didn't matter. But Bernice *killed* herself because she loved me so!"[24]

In Act Two, Margaret learns from Abbie that Bernice died of natural causes; she did not kill herself but requested that Abbie tell Craig that she did. Margaret interprets this as a vengeful attempt to devastate unfaithful Craig with guilt, an act that indicates that Bernice's "life was *hate*" (206). So disillusioned is Margaret that she refuses to enter the bedroom where Bernice lies. In Act Three, Margaret sees that Bernice's gesture has indeed improved Craig since he renounces his world of "make-believe" (226) and insists on rearranging the room as Bernice always kept it. Margaret realizes that Bernice's true motive was to remove Craig's insecurity by giving him a sense of how valued he was, so the play ends with Bernice remaining the paragon that almost everyone considers her.

"Saint" *Bernice* is a curiously defensive play, as if Glaspell protests too much the transcendent goodness of her heroine. Although she seems to present Bernice as a martyr and saint, the cost of her canonization seems too high: in a brief reference at the beginning of Act Two, Abbie says that Bernice died of stomach ulcers (180); she may well have been killed by repressed anger, the good girl's disease. The play's uncomfortable sense of conflicting messages may emanate from Glaspell's own confusions, as Marcia Noe speculates:

> *Bernice* may be more easily understood if viewed in the context of Susan Glaspell's life with Jig Cook, who, like Craig Norris, was unfaithful to his wife and, much of the time, unsuccessful as a writer. Could *Bernice* have grown from a fantasy of Susan's in which she killed herself to punish Jig for his infidelity, all the while rationalizing that the act would bring him to his senses and shock him into living up to his potential as a writer?[25]

Noe's explanation seems plausible since Bernice does seem to be indulging in the behavior of a petulant child who threatens, "You'll be sorry when I run away." Glaspell may also be attempting to reassure herself about her childless state in that Bernice has also suffered a stillbirth, as well as about her choice of a career as an artist rather than a social reformer. She may be asking woman's traditional guilty question: Have I done enough for others or have I actually devoted too much attention to myself? Glaspell presents her defense of Bernice, and herself, through the contrasting lives of the other women characters as well as through their refracted composite portrait of Bernice.

Through the character of Laura, Glaspell defends Bernice against her failure to become a conventional wife and mother. Laura is the only character in the play who does not revere Bernice; instead she blames her for not having "the power to hold Craig" (186) from straying and for failing to "value Craig's work" (188). Laura is the kind of woman who wants other women to be as miserable as she is in order to validate her suffering. Despite her limited perspective, she has a moment of insight when she is attempting to help organize Bernice's funeral and comments, "Really I do like control" (209). Her drive for autonomy must find its channel, limited though it is.

Clearly, Bernice should not have joined Laura in deformed domesticity, but Margaret's career presents a more problematic alternative. Like many of Glaspell's Greenwich Village friends, Margaret is a social reformer; she currently works in Chicago, "trying to get out of prison all those people who are imprisoned for ideas" (187). However commendable Margaret's goals, she is shown to have made the poorer choice because, as she tells Craig, "We give ourselves in fighting for a thing that seems important and in that fight we get out of the flow of life. We had meant it to deepen the flow—but we get caught" (198). Since Bernice's dying word was Margaret's name, she clearly means to get Margaret back into that flow by causing her to perceive and appreciate what the play presents as a totally unselfish act, her last message to Craig. Margaret is like a disciple who has her faith tested in order to prove herself a worthy successor to the apotheosized Bernice, and Margaret's final words show that she has succeeded: "Oh, in all the world—since life first *moved*—has there been any beauty like the beauty of perceiving love? . . . No, not for words" (230).

The emotional core of the play, though, resides in Bernice's attempt to defend herself against the charge of thwarting Craig's potential by failing to surrender her very soul to him. Craig regards marriage as a power struggle from which the man should emerge the victorious master of his slave-object-wife; he comments that Bernice had "a life in her deeper than anything that could be done to her. . . . I never *had* Bernice" (173). He childishly justifies his affairs as attempts to gain her exclusive attention: "A man's feeling is different. He has to feel that he moves—completely moves—yes, could destroy—not that he would, but has the power to reshape the—" (174). Margaret perceptively tells him, "Those love affairs of yours—they're like your false writing—to keep yourself from knowing that you haven't power" (200). Craig is supposedly redeemed when Bernice lets him believe he had enough power to make her take the role of abandoned wife and kill herself in jealousy and grief. The play suggests that Bernice has proven herself a "true woman" in rescuing Craig, but the rescue is based on a lie, as if men cannot bear too much reality.

Glaspell not only defends Bernice against putative lapses as conventional woman and social reformer, but asserts her virtues as a mother, though without biological children, and as an artist, despite her lack of a tangible medium. Bernice mothers everyone: as we have seen, from the grave she nurtures Craig and Margaret; when alive, she cared for her childish and withdrawn father and guided and inspired her servant Abbie, played by Glaspell in the original production. Abbie seems to glory in her self-abdication, like a child who wants to please and emulate what she perceives as the perfect mother or master: "It was the *main* thing in my life— doing what she wanted" (164). In some ways, the unsatisfactorily ethereal Bernice and dog-like Abbie become more palatable if one regards them as complements who together form a whole. Bernice thinks and inspires while Abbie acts and confronts the consequences. Glaspell, however, seems unable to create such a complete woman in this play unless it is Margaret, who at the final curtain has learned from Bernice and Abbie to rekindle the vision that will make her activism meaningful.

A more positive way to view Bernice may be as a sort of Henry Jamesian artist-in-life, like Milly Theale in *The Wings of the Dove* or Maggie Verver in *The Golden Bowl*, who uses life as a medium to create beauty and wholeness, often at significant cost to herself.

As Sharon P. Friedman aptly observes, "Bernice has imagined and executed the scenario from which the drama emerges."[26] C.W.E. Bigsby sees this staging as a form of female empowerment, "one in which the determining voice and actions are those of women who deliberately create the dramas within which men are obliged to act."[27] Bernice has not produced biological children or artistic artifacts, but her legacy to the future, through Craig the artist and Margaret the reformer, will help promote human evolution, the process that Glaspell considered of paramount importance, much as do Mrs. Patrick and Allie Mayo in *The Outside* and the Woman from Idaho in *The People*. That may be Glaspell's ostensible or intended theme, but her subtext works against it since, to return to the Jamesian analogy, like Milly Theale, Bernice is dead and, like Maggie Verver, the valorization of her marriage is based on unacknowledged deceit.

Glaspell's last major Provincetown plays, *Inheritors* (1921) and *The Verge* (1921), continue to explore the nonbiologically maternal roles of social reformer and artist while examining the influence of biological mothers, for good or ill, upon their daughters. The cultivation of new types of plants is the central metaphor in both plays, suggesting that the development of the species, or offspring, may come only at great cost to the gardener, already a mutant-mother herself.

In *The Road to the Temple*, Glaspell comments that "new country is a good place to look at society. When you see grandfather, father and son you see human society, with personal quality, luck and changing conditions making destiny." Glaspell returns to the Midwest in *Inheritors* for the purpose of examining two "species" over time, the Fejevary and Morton families, but with just as much emphasis on the maternal as the paternal line.[28] In Act One, on the Fourth of July, 1879, Silas Morton decides to promote intellectual independence by donating a beautiful and valuable hill on his farm for the site of a new college, despite the objections of his mother and the cash of a land-developer. One of his motives was his own regret over his lack of education, a deficiency he realized from the society of his cultivated best friend, the aristocratic Hungarian immigrant Felix Fejevary, a liberty-loving revolutionary forced to flee his native land.

Act Two takes place in 1920, as if Glaspell intends it for a warning to chauvinistic postwar America. Felix Fejevary II, son of the immigrant, is now president of Morton College, and he is discovered in the college library reassuring an influential state senator that such subversive elements as Professor Holden will be silenced so that the senate will appropriate large sums for the college. He is distracted from his machinations by the sound of a fracas outside. Fejevary's son Horace, a jingoistic student, has tried to silence two student demonstrators from India. When the police saw trouble beginning, they grabbed the darker-skinned students somewhat roughly. Horace's cousin and fellow student Madeleine, granddaughter of Silas Morton and the first Felix Fejevary, rushed impulsively to the Indians' aid and hit the policeman with her tennis racket.

Acts Three and Four concern Madeleine's gradual realization that her spontaneous blow for freedom is really her true inheritance from the past and her wisest course for the future. In Act Three, President Fejevary is again busily selling out freedom of speech in the ironic setting of the library as he threatens to dismiss Professor Holden unless he stops protesting the mistreatment of Fred Jordan, a former student who is imprisoned for his unpopular conscientious objection to the recent war. Fejevary's threat is particularly nasty since Holden is the sole support of an invalid wife. Fejevary is once more interrupted in his sleazy activities by Madeleine, this time as she defends her action because the Indian students are "people from the other side of the world who came here believing in us, drawn from the far side of the world by things we say about ourselves."[29] She hears a new uproar involving the Indian students and rushes out to rejoin the fray as the act's curtain descends.

In Act Four, a week after her arrest, Madeleine holds to her resolve to go to prison, like Fred Jordan, rather than deny her beliefs, despite the pleas of her father Ira, her Aunt Isabel, the vanquished Professor Holden, and the possible love interest of Emil Johnson. Madeleine's move from the tennis court to the police court may seem rather abrupt. Why isn't Madeleine more like her fellow students and foils, Doris and Fussie, whose idea of a good time is making fun of a farm boy by pretending to be infatuated with him? Glaspell has, however, carefully prepared us for Madeleine's difference by her portraits of Madeleine's female ancestors and their foils, suggesting that women of every generation have the potential to be pioneers and further humanity's development, though in quite different ways.

Silas Morton's mother, called Grandmother in Act One, is a literal pioneer. Interestingly, no mention is made of Silas' deceased wife, rebellious Madeleine's actual grandmother, as if to give schematic emphasis to the first generation of pioneers. Grandmother fought the Indians singlehandedly when she was attacked, once throwing one into her cellar and standing on the door, but she also could befriend them, trading cookies for fish, because she understands their motivation: "We roiled them up considerable. They was mostly friendly when let be. Didn't want to give up their land — but I've noticed something of the same nature in white folks" (104). Grandmother also identifies with another marginalized group, her fellow women. She tells the first Felix Fejevary that when she left the house, she would always leave some food for the settlers stopping for a respite before proceeding further west. Her longing for sisterly companionship is manifest as she tells him,

> There was a woman I always wanted to know. She made a kind of bread I never had before — and left a-plenty for our supper when we got back with the ducks and berries. And she left the kitchen handier than it had ever been. I often wondered about her — where she came from, and where she went (107).

This memory is another version of *Trifles* in that one woman speculates about another through examining her housekeeping, but in this instance to be inspired by her strength, not chastened by her destruction.

Despite her empathy as a young woman, in her senescence Grandmother tries to prevent Silas from deeding the hill to the college, exclaiming, "I worked for that hill! And I tell you to leave it to your own children!" (115). Her foil is the cultured Old Mrs. Fejevary who "did have an awful ladylike way of feeding the chickens" (106). Through Grandmother, Glaspell is indicating that the very virtues that promote pioneering, courageous visioning, and industry are so strenuous that they can only be sustained for a limited duration without intellectual and cultural resources like those of Old Mrs. Fejevary; the solitary and untutored pioneer soon slips back into the narrow nurturing of her own family, rather than the human family.

The next generation also contains two contrasting women. Madeleine's Aunt Isabel, wife of the second Felix, is a woman who is very warm and caring toward her family and her own kind but is unable to empathize with those who are different. In a statement typical of the era's xenophobia, she tells her niece, "These are days when we have to stand together — all of us who are the same kind of people must stand together because the thing that makes us the same kind of people is threatened" (147).

Fortunately, Madeleine has a more generous female role model, her deceased mother, Madeleine Fejevary Morton, sister of President Fejevary. Young Madeleine initially knows very little of her mother since her widowed father Ira finds the subject so painful. On the day of her twenty-first birthday, the day she must turn herself into the judge, Madeleine makes some fudge in an attempt to celebrate her birthday by herself since she is alienated from her family. She later tells her Aunt Isabel,

> And then that didn't seem to — make a birthday, so I happened to see this [a Hungarian dish], way up on a top shelf, and I remembered that it was my mother's. It was nice to get it down and use it — almost as if mother was giving me a birthday present (147).

Madeleine does receive a present from her mother through the unlikely mediation of her father Ira, a fanatical developer of a new breed of corn, who, in Grandmother and Isabel's way, refuses to share it with other farmers. As he tries to prevent Madeleine from choosing prison, Ira tells her how her mother died.

> Then *she* came — that ignorant Swede, Emil Johnson's mother — running through the cornfield like a crazy woman — "Miss Morton! Miss Morton! Come help me! My children are choking!" Diphtheria they had — the whole of 'em — but out of this house she ran — my Madeleine, leaving you — her own baby — running as fast as she could through the cornfield after that ignorant woman. . . . That was the last I saw of her. She choked to death in that Swede's house. They lived (154).

Madeleine proves herself her mother's daughter when she decides to hurt her family for their and America's ultimate good by standing up for her principles, no matter what the cost.

Like the corn that Ira Morton grows, Madeleine combines the best of her different strains, the Mortons' hard work and neighborliness and the Fejevarys' cultural breadth and rebelliousness. She could also be regarded as a kind of mutant, and in the human world, such pioneers can be rejected and destroyed for their difference, no matter what benefits humanity may ultimately reap from them.

Madeleine may gain strength from challenging the system, but she could be willfully choosing her self-destruction in an oppressive world, as does Claire Archer in *The Verge*. Early in the play, Claire's husband Harry humorously comments upon Claire's blunt language: "This is what came of the men who made the laws that made New England, that here is the flower of those gentleman of culture."[30] Harry will learn, however, that this is no beneficent plant like Ira's corn, but a monstrous mutant formed by the pressures of patriarchal strictures on a venturesome and creative woman.[31]

Claire, like Ira Morton, expresses her autonomy and creativity through her plants, and, also like Ira, she is jealous of her private space, the greenhouse that she considers her room of her own; she even tells her husband, "I'll not have you in my place!" (61). She describes one of her experiments, the Breath of Life plant, to her lover Dick:

> I want to give fragrance to Breath of Life—the flower I have created that is outside where flowers have been. What has gone out should bring fragrance from what it has left. But no definite fragrance, no limiting enclosing thing. I call the fragrance I am trying to create Reminiscence. Reminiscent of the rose, the violet, arbutus—but a new thing—itself. Breath of Life may be lonely out in what hasn't been. Perhaps someday I can give it reminiscence (63–64).

As her close friend Tom, an explorer, perceives, "If she can do it with plants, perhaps she won't have to do it with herself" (71). Unfortunately, as in the case of Mrs. Patrick and Allie Mayo in *The Outside*, watching plants, whether they are scrubby beach bushes or Breath of Life, will not suffice, for Claire wants to be a woman on "the outside" or "the verge."[32]

Mrs. Patrick is perceived as monstrous by the lifesavers for her bitter reclusiveness and at least initially by the audience for her attempt to bar the drowning man from her house. Glaspell presents Claire Archer as similarly armored in her own problems. Even at the beginning of the play, she does not care about the comfort or feelings of others. On a frigid, snowy day, she has all the house's heat directed to the greenhouse to preserve her plants and then objects when her husband and guests wish to breakfast there, a gesture that at first seems a comic eccentricity but by the play's end can be seen as part of Claire's willed withdrawal from others.

Glaspell is not unproblematically presenting Claire as a monster of egotism since the men who surround her, the representative Tom, Dick, and Harry, do not seem worthy of much serious attention. Her husband Harry just wants a wife who will be the life of the party so he tries to fit her horticultural experiments into a suitably feminine paradigm: "That's an awfully nice thing for a woman to do—raise flowers" (65). Her lover Dick just wants his ego boosted by a beautiful woman who belongs to another man; he dismisses her experiments as "merely the excess of a particularly rich temperament" (65). The man who does understand her experiments, the ironically named explorer Tom Edgeworthy, is unwilling to risk the challenge of an experimental relationship with Claire; he is about to run away on his next journey to avoid exploring his own or Claire's inner space. When he offers to keep Claire "safe" (99), she is momentarily lured, but then shoots him because, as she says, "I'd rather be the steam rising from the manure than be a thing called beautiful!" (99).

Glaspell not only presents a heroine who rejects her assigned role as man's plaything, but challenges an even more basic cultural assumption, the unwavering, self-sacrificial devotion of a mother for her child. In an ironic reversal of the usual intergenerational scene, Claire rejects Elizabeth, her daughter from a previous marriage, because she is *not* a rebel. The now-adult Elizabeth recalls an "idol" given to her mother by Tom: "I dressed the idol up in my doll's clothes. They fitted perfectly—the idol was just the size of my doll Ailine. But mother didn't like the idol that way, and tore the clothes getting them off" (73). Claire is authoritarian in her denial of Elizabeth's play, conventional though the child's game may be. She does not explain her reasons to Elizabeth, but remains inarticulately violent and destructive, caring more about her own sense of appropriateness than about her daughter's treasured doll-clothes.

This remembered scene aptly foreshadows Claire's total rejection of the grown Elizabeth, who, unsurprisingly, received the remainder of her upbringing from Claire's traditional sister Adelaide. When Elizabeth arrives after a year's absence and tries to "embrace" her mother, Claire defensively holds a box that she is carrying in front of her and says, "Careful, Elizabeth. We mustn't upset the lice" (74), though she apparently considers it acceptable to upset her own daughter. Claire compares her other great experiment, the Edge Vine, to Elizabeth, telling her, "I should destroy the Edge Vine. It isn't — over the edge. It's running, back to — 'all the girls'" (77). At the end of the scene, she does try to uproot the Edge Vine, exclaiming, "Why did I make you? To get past you!" (78). She strikes Elizabeth with the vine and declares, "To think that object ever moved my belly and sucked my breast" (78).

This scene is shocking today, but in 1921 it must have been even more so to the recent heirs of Victorian mother-worship for whom Adelaide appears to speak when she upbraids her sister Claire, "A mother who does not love her own child! You are an unnatural woman" (85). Again, though, Glaspell complicates her portrait of Claire as a monster, a Medea, when Claire later tells Tom about her son by Harry who died when he was a small child.

> I was up with Harry — flying — high. It was about four months before David was born — the doctor was furious — pregnant women are supposed to keep to earth. We were going fast — I *was* flying — I had left the earth. And then — within me, movement, for the first time — stirred to life far in air — movement within. The man unborn, he too, would fly. And so — I always loved him. He was movement — and wonder. In his short life were many flights. I never told anyone about the last one. His little bed was by the window — he wasn't four years old. It was night, but him not asleep. He saw the morning star — you know — the morning star. Brighter — stranger — reminiscent-and a promise. He pointed " — Mother," he asked me, "what is there — beyond the stars?" A baby, a sick baby — the morning star. Next night — the finger that pointed was — (*suddenly bites her own finger*) But, yes, I am glad. He would have tried to move and too much would hold him. Wonder would die — and he'd laugh at soaring (87).

Claire expected David to "soar" for her since he was a male and "pregnant women are supposed to keep to earth."[33] In *Of Woman Born*, Adrienne Rich describes a similar expectation.

I wanted to give birth, at twenty-five, to my unborn self, the self that our father-centered family had suppressed in me, someone independent, actively willing, original — those possibilities I had felt in myself in flashes as a young student and writer, and from which, during pregnancy, I was to close myself off. If I wanted to give birth to myself as a male, it was because males seemed to inherit those qualities by right of gender.[34]

Unlike Claire, though, Rich went on to raise three sons, participate in the feminist movement of the 1960s, and do her own soaring herself as expressed in her great poetry.

Some forty years earlier, Claire sees her own option for vicarious accomplishment closed by her son's premature death, and even wonders if such a repressive society would allow male self-expression since "too much would hold him." Claire tries to express herself through her plants, fails, and ends the play as a mad murderess, singing "Nearer My God to Thee." When we seek an explanation for Claire's debacle, her lack of a feminist sisterhood is a necessary but not sufficient cause. Linda Ben-Zvi provides the essential difference between Claire and Rich, and Claire and Glaspell, when she writes,

Since [Glaspell's] women are exploring new areas of their lives, they find traditional language unsuited to their needs. They may be women unused to speech or women all too aware that the words they speak do not express their thoughts. In either case, the results are the same. Her characters are virtually inarticulate, or are rendered so because of the situations in which they find themselves. The most common punctuation mark she uses is the dash. It is used when the character is unsure of the direction in which she is going, as yet unprepared to articulate consciously a new awareness or unwilling to put into words feelings and wishes which may collapse under the weight of words.[35]

Because they cannot speak, many of them act self-destructively: Minnie Wright, Mrs. Patrick, Allie Mayo, Bernice Norris, Madeleine Fejevary, and Claire Archer.

Almost all of Glaspell's heroines are, in one sense or another, childless: Minnie, the Woman from Idaho, Mrs. Patrick, Allie Mayo, the Scorned One, the Cheated One, Bernice, Madeleine, and Claire. They are also artists without viable mediums of expression. Minnie Wright expects her canary to sing for her; The Woman from

Idaho wants to inspire the Editor to write for her; the six women in *Woman's Honor* can only protest their situations, in effect save their own lives, through saving the life of a foolish male-chauvinist; Mrs. Patrick and Allie Mayo see the stunted vegetation on the outside of Cape Cod as their living symbol; Bernice uses her death to make changes she could not achieve by living; Madeleine Morton expresses her sense of injustice by hitting a policeman and will presumably be imprisoned; and Claire Archer, thwarted by patriarchy, the death of her son, and the failure of her daughter and her plants, projects her own rage one step further by shooting a man and imprisoning herself in her own madness.

None of these heroines seem to have Glaspell's own outlet for her creative, maternal passions, her artistry with words and structure. This may be depressing, but it is realistic, for how many women, or, for that matter, men, are so gifted? The hope lies in Glaspell's speech, her maternal legacy to that better future in which she so fervently believed. The agonized voices, and silences, of her women on the edge, are, as Allie Mayo hesitantly declaims in her last speech of the play, the "stunted straggly line that meets the Outside face to face — and fights for what itself can never be. Lonely line. Brave growing" (116).

5

Whose Life Is It Anyway?
The Road to the Temple

In her plays, some of Glaspell's women on "the outside" have female friends or supporters, like the band of women at the end of *Woman's Honor* or the nascent alliance between Allie Mayo and Mrs. Patrick in *The Outside*. The isolated and alienated women, such as Minnie Wright in *Trifles* and Claire Archer in *The Verge*, are the desperate ones. Glaspell, unfortunately, was to join the latter group when George Cram Cook decided to abandon the too-successful Provincetown Players for a new experiment. In order to accompany her husband to Greece in 1922, she had to renounce the kindred spirits of Greenwich Village's Heterodoxy Club and Provincetown friends like novelist Neith Boyce. Although Cook believed he was entering his true homeland, Glaspell did not even speak the language. With her usual cheerful determination, she tried to regard this deracination positively. Ironically, she did not consider her great plays her true work and thought of her Greek sojourn as an opportunity to return to her own genre, fiction, since she had published no novels since *Fidelity* in 1915. As she wrote to her mother, "The theater has always made it hard for me to write and now I will have a better chance for my own writing."[1]

Glaspell would not publish another novel until *Brook Evans* in 1928, but this period was neither idle nor an idyll. Through great trials, particularly Cook's unexpected death in 1924, she came to terms with her personal and working relationship with Cook. The progress of her spiritual and geographical pilgrimage can be seen in four works of varying lengths and genres: a brief essay for the *New Republic*, "Dwellers on Parnassos" (1923); a hagiographic memoir of Cook she wrote as a preface to her collection of his poems, "Last Days in Greece" in *Greek Coins* (1925); a short story, "The Faithless Shepherd" (1926); and a biography of Cook, *The Road to the Temple* (1927).[2]

None of these pieces are autobiographies in the commonly accepted sense of the term since all focus on Cook. One naturally wonders why Glaspell did not write an autobiography since she certainly had a story to tell: poor Midwestern girl becomes famous writer, joins the Greenwich Village avant garde, co-founds the Provincetown Players, and sojourns by the Delphic Oracle. In many ways her tale is more interesting than that of Cook who started life with many advantages and seemed to do largely as he pleased. Glaspell's overcoming of obstacles would be more dramatic, suspenseful, and satisfying, all qualities she recognized and valued as a skilled writer.

By all accounts, though, Glaspell was a kind, considerate, reticent person who, unlike Cook, acted as though she did not need or expect center stage. In other words, she was ladylike, and for such women, as Carolyn G. Heilbrun states in *Writing a Woman's Life*,

> Identity is grounded through relation to the chosen other. Without such relation, women do not feel able to write openly about themselves; even with it, they do not feel entitled to credit for their own accomplishment, spiritual or not.[3]

Sidonie Smith provides an additional explanation for Glaspell's failure to write a formal autobiography when she characterizes some pre-modern women autobiographers:

> If she pursues a self-representation structured in the fictions of goodness and self-effacement, she remains silenced, literally as she gives the world a book it will bother to read and symbolically as she reenacts woman's role as the mediator of man's life, a passive sign to be passed around in patriarchal fictions. Literally, she can write no formal autobiography.[4]

Instead, Glaspell writes what Susan Groag Bell and Marilyn Yalom call "autobiography masquerading as biography."[5] Despite her ostensible focus on Cook, Glaspell is telling her own story; she is the author, and these pieces are her works, not Cook's; we are presented with her portrait of Cook, not Cook himself.

"Dwellers on Parnassos," less than three pages long, encapsulates Glaspell's conflicting attitudes toward Greece and Cook. She wants to believe with Cook that Greece is Eden, a refuge from the modern world, but the acuteness of her observations always prevents her from lingering in a pastoral mode. The piece starts as this sort of paradise lost: the materialistic American, Glaspell, seems to receive her comeuppance when she offers to pay for some cheese a shepherd had brought her, not realizing that it was intended as a gift. Glaspell feels "unworthy of my place of residence" (188), but she later learns from the shepherd that he does expect a form of payment: he wants Glaspell to state in her book that "on Parnassos lives a shepherd, Elias Skarmoothes, and that this man is a good shepherd, and your friend" (188). She tries to reconcile her conflicting ideal and reality by asking, "Why beware of Greeks bearing gifts when they bear them so beautifully, and will quite ingenuously let you know their expectations?" (188).

The shepherd here stands for a patriarchal society in both its pastoral and modern phases. Glaspell and Cook are invited to feast with the shepherd; idyllically, he roasts lamb while they recline on spruce boughs. Glaspell becomes horrified when the shepherd's two-year-old grandson falls asleep from too much wine. When she suggests that milk might be better for the toddler, "the shepherd grew tremendous in his pride, saying his child would not touch milk and that the insensible infant's grandfather, similarly reared, had the day before, aged ninety, walked three hours up the mountain" (188). Glaspell next witnesses modern machismo in action when she sees Greek refugees returning to Salonika from war-torn Asia Minor. She sees many victims of this male war, but seems particularly moved by "the mothers walking along with tired children they have no place to put to bed. Curious how they keep on walking—as if with the idea it must be better somewhere else" (200). Glaspell plainly does not share their belief since the essay ends with an image of an absentee, uncaring, patriarchal god: "In a panic, in great terror, the whole flock is running! The shepherd on the summit—we've not yet heard from him" (200).

By the time Glaspell published *Greek Coins* in 1925, her own shepherd was dead and buried at Delphi, and this collection of

Cook's poems, "With Memorabilia by Floyd Dell, Edna Kenton, and Susan Glaspell," is her first attempt to build a monument for him to replace the tomb she left behind in Greece. Glaspell orders the front matter in biographically traditional chronological order: Dell discusses Iowa, Kenton treats the theater days, and Glaspell recounts the "Last Days in Greece." All of these "memorabilia," including her own, leave Glaspell out, as if only by excluding her can Cook appear to full advantage. Indeed, on the first page of "A Seer in Iowa," Dell forgets Glaspell, sighing, "If only among these companions there had been a Plato to give him his due immortality."[6] Dell is trying to beg Cook's relative lack of tangible, durable accomplishments by stressing his inspirational, charismatic nature, as so strikingly manifested in his conversation.

In "Provincetown and MacDougal Street," Kenton erases Glaspell's achievement as a playwright as she presents what she regards as a talismanic moment: "I have that picture of him standing on the sea-backed stage at Provincetown, telling me of the new great playwright to be [Eugene O'Neill], of the new great plays we were to produce."[7] Kenton sees Cook exclusively as a male-midwife to male genius. She also depicts herself as a historian, "fairly impersonally interested" (19), and Cook as the Great Man who changes the course of history since "his was the single spirit dedicated wholly to the [Provincetown] experiment" (22). She does shade his portrait, though, when she relates the way he defied the vote of the Provincetown Players and spent most of their funds on a dome for their production of O'Neill's *The Emperor Jones*. Perhaps out of respect for the eulogistic nature of the volume, she papers over this affront to democracy, calling it "an outstanding example of fine dictatorship as to purpose and, as fate would have it, to result as well" (26), so that the means justify the ends.

Dell and Kenton's memorabilia illustrate the difficulties in writing about Cook. How does one convey greatness when very little evidence of it remains and the great man could be as much an obsessive egotist as a catalytic shaman? In "Last Days in Greece," Glaspell does so by sweeping negative evidence under the rug as she depicts herself as a happy disciple, who, like the apostles, would occasionally express a doubt or ask a question, but would be set straight by the Messiah, Cook. On the first page, she says of his decision to go to Greece, "It was a call — the call to his promised land. Something in his spirit knew he was through with what he had been doing" (31), and he went about his father's (patriarchy's) business.[8]

Her method of furthering Cook's apotheosis is exemplified in this anecdote of his building a wall at their summer camp at Kalania.

> He loved the old walls of Greece; he loved building his own wall, and he built well. But there was his play of Delphi to write, a play of noble sweep, already a living thing in him. So, wife-like, I would at times protest about day after day being given to moving stones. One day I said the quite banal thing, "Why, it isn't even our own place. We may never see it again." And he answered: "It's part of the earth. So beautiful it deserves to be made beautiful. If every man would shape one small part of his world, think what the earth would become" (43).

To highlight Cook as Christ, she must play doubting Thomas in the guise of a stereotypically shrewish, grasping, and obtuse wife; her speech must appear silly to make his actions appear less futile. This strategy is a reversal of a nineteenth-century British mode by which women claimed "authorship" and "self-authorship" by writing the lives of famous male relations.[9] In contrast, Glaspell was already an acclaimed novelist and playwright; she seems to play the handmaiden's role in order to make Cook seem as if he were a great man.

Further, in "Last Days in Greece," Glaspell even sugarcoats the aspects of Cook's behavior that she found most difficult to accept. When Cook is childishly disappointed to find the Eiffel Tower depicted on his egg cup at the inn at Delphi, Glaspell comments, "I feared life at the Pythian Apollo would not move smoothly after this rejection of the Eiffel Tower" (36). Her humorous tone is meant to decoy the reader from how hard it must have been to keep the mercurial and demanding Cook placated. As her letters indicate, Glaspell deeply resented the way Cook would neglect her for most of a day by drinking with the men.[10] In "Last Days in Greece," though, she proclaims, "Those were great nights in Andreas Koryls's wineshop in Delphi, when Jig Cook drank the wine of Parnassos with villagers and shepherds, listened to their stories and opened to them their own great past" (39). Glaspell seems oblivious to the way the educated foreigner patronizes the "ignorant" villagers about their own culture.

At the end of "Last Days in Greece," Glaspell's hagiography dissipates into the ludicrous because the facts do not match her tone. Cook died of glanders, which he contracted from a pet dog, but, for Glaspell, this is the crucifixion: "The man who all his life loved and understood dogs gave his life for one of them" (46). In the last lines of the piece, he even has a sort of resurrection in that, entombed in Greece, "it is as if the gods know their own. . . . And it is the ages have taken him — his life beautiful as a spruce tree seen jaggedly black against the evening sky" (49). "Last Days in Greece" epitomizes what Heilbrun calls "the old genre of female autobiography, which tends to find beauty even in pain and to transform rage into spiritual acceptance."[11]

Although Glaspell may seem to be enacting the role of Ernestine Hubers in *The Glory of the Conquered*, who sets her work aside to complete that of her husband, her arrangement and selection of his poems is much more honest than her eulogistic preface. She begins with "Though Stone Be Broken," a poem written in their courtship, when he was married to Mollie Price, so that Glaspell was "Love, dearest love, whom bitter barriers keep/In loneliness afar" (59). This is not a conventional love poem because Cook professes his devotion to the abstraction Love, not love as embodied in one woman: "Loves fail: the unshaken soul of us makes sure/That Love shall not" (58); this may well be a warning to Glaspell of philanderings to come, rationalized by a higher law.

Cook's poems reveal that he believes he has such privileges because he is a man. In "Georgic," he presents his Great Chain of Being:

> The sexual clutch of myriads of men,
> The pain of women bringing forth their young,
> The crunch of ancient jaws on screaming prey,
> The blood of animals who held life dear,
> The juice primeval plants sucked . . . (70).

Men can "clutch," and their women pay the consequences in "pain," but after all, women rank only just above the savage animals and "primeval plants." Cook dislikes Christ as a representation of divinity because he considers his passivity feminine, and femininity equals masochism, as he writes in "Meditation on Gods": "Hating the will to destroy/This god embodied a more feminine will/To be destroyed" (95). Women were assigned another passive role in "I Woke from Sleep."

> I dare not sleep alone longer lest the universe perish.
> You must wake by my side hereafter, beloved.
> You are the white meaning of life (76).

Women are apparently good for something other than the "sexual clutch"; they can sacrifice sleep in order to serve as witnesses to deity and vessels of meaning.

Cook's desperate refusal to exchange youth's ecstasy for the wisdom of age is also evident in these poems. In "From My Old Age," he rages like the elderly Yeats:

> I, old man, hate, the old-world.
> I have no more use for it, no more sympathy with
>   it, no more temperament of it, than I had when
>   I was twenty (90).

In "At Fifty I Ask God," he identifies his true lover as God and his fellow men as "this lice-like human world," and asks,

> Why, knowing me, being my lover,
> Have you not made me blow
> Their pismire spirit into atoms? (125).

This verges on megalomania since Cook wants to deny aging, one of the life-processes to which he has always claimed such devotion.

The frontispiece of *Greek Coins* is a photograph of a Greek shepherd, but it is actually George Cram Cook in the shepherd's garb that he loved to wear in his last days in Delphi. From this picture one might argue that he was no longer the man Glaspell had married, but he was, only more so. Glaspell seems to recognize the inevitability of their estrangement in the poem about last things that she places last, "That Winter Day," in which the poet and his lover, "lingering," watch a sunset. It concludes:

> As the moon draws the sea I felt a power
> As of all planets drawing me to her,
> Infinite stress and yet I did not stir
> Nor touch her hand (136).

For all her valiant efforts to depict Cook as a god-like creator and inspirer in "Last Days in Greece," the poems show him to be a man who believes he is god-like and who is embittered and alienated when neither god nor "the lice-like human world" acknowledges it.

By the next year, 1926, whether due to distance in time and space or her new liaison with a younger man, Norman Matson, Glaspell was ready to present a more critical yet still sympathetic portrait of Cook in her short story "The Faithless Shepherd." Epimonondas Paraskeva is the son of a shepherd. Although he begins to learn the alphabet from the village priest and can identify the letters in "Dionysos" carved in the temple at Delphi, his father insists that he has no need for letters since he will be a shepherd. Deflected from the ironically Apollonian studies that might lead him to Dionysian ecstasies, he turns to nature for mystic raptures in the beautiful valley of Kalania that was "a heart guarded by mountains of spruce" (55). Neither he nor life is sufficiently perfect to sustain such communion beyond a transcendent moment, so he tries to repeat the ecstasy through getting drunk with the villagers, but "they passed it, they did not know the moment when it was theirs. It would end in Epimonondas Paraskeva becoming more quarrelsome than any" (57).

Epimonondas becomes increasingly despondent when the girl whom he loves wants to marry a shopkeeper who has been to America and wears modern clothes. For sanity he clings to his sheep with a maternal feeling. "He thought of the flock as one, as gentle life that moved on the mountain, its helplessness his own reason for being" (58) and hopes "that over him too was that which knew the doom that waited, and with rejoicing made by sorrow loved keeping him safe in his moment of gladness" (59). In his impatience for mystic ecstasy, he moves his flock to Kalania too early in the season so that they sicken. "He was held there with the flock he could not move as a mother with a sick child" (64). In his guilt he becomes an outlaw but cannot bring himself to kill another shepherd who has betrayed the outlaws because, though that shepherd had never experienced the mystic ecstasy, he faithfully cared for his sheep. "He, the bad shepherd who knew many other things, loved the good shepherd who knew only his sheep" (70). Epimonondas returns to Kalania where he is killed by another outlaw and dies writing the final letters in the name Dionysos. As in "Dwellers in Parnassos," the ultimate Good Shepherd is once again absent.

In "The Faithless Shepherd" Glaspell is questioning whether mystic ecstasy is worth the price one pays for it and, more importantly, what one makes others pay for it. Is not the shepherd's first duty to his flock? Living as if every man were an island is unrealistic and makes one a faithless shepherd. Glaspell does show some ambivalence here: she admires Epimonondas-Cook's drive and his inability to compromise, but she also sees it as a selfishness that can destroy the self as well as innocent bystanders. She could have called the story "The Faithful Shepherd" if she wanted to suggest that the shepherd was faithful to a higher ideal, but she calls him "faithless" as if she is declaring that charity begins at home.

Glaspell's final attempt to appraise Cook is *The Road to the Temple* (1927), a work that has puzzled critics since its publication.[12] Part of the problem is the vexed question of genre. It is not an autobiography in the traditional sense since Cook, not Glaspell, is ostensibly the central figure. *The Road to the Temple* is not a memoir since Glaspell's own experiences with Cook do not begin until he is past thirty, midway through the book; it is not a life history since she is not transcribing his oral account of his life; and it is not a biography in the modern sense of a somewhat objective account based on extensive research and documentation.[13] The older, more subjective, type of biography is a closer fit since one could make the comparison that Dell did not: Glaspell could be the Plato to Cook's Socrates, but the gender difference is important to Glaspell's account. Glaspell and Cook could also be compared to Boswell and Johnson, but Glaspell is the more accomplished figure of the two, and that is another significant factor in her narrative.

Some of the difficulty arises from the attempt to shoehorn *The Road to the Temple* into the paradigms of masculine lifewriting. In *The Tradition of Women's Autobiography: From Antiquity to the Present*, Estelle C. Jelinek presents a paradigm in which *The Road to the Temple* would fit if Glaspell and Cook are considered as the complementary halves of a whole person or subject. First, women's autobiography stresses "personal matters": Cook is a public great man to Glaspell, but she focuses on his inner strivings, intellectual and spiritual, not events, facts, and dates. Second, in

their autobiographies, women present "a multidimensional, fragmented self-image colored by a sense of inadequacy and alienation": Cook often felt frustrated that he could not achieve his
goals, but he always believed his struggle to be central, not mar-
ginal, while Glaspell, on the other hand, for all her authorial competence, was often marginalized and appears in the book only in
fragments. Finally, women's autobiographies are "episodic and
anecdotal, nonchronological and disjunctive": *The Road to the
Temple* is roughly chronological and linear in the tradition of
male autobiography, befitting Cook, but Glaspell changes style
and structure within and between chapters and flashes forward and
back as she sees fit.[14]

In a sense, *The Road to the Temple* fits an earlier model of
composite auto/biography. Jelinek writes that in the seventeenth
century, "it was a common practice for women to write portraits
of their esteemed husbands or other male relatives of stature, to
which they then appended, with appropriate modesty, a briefer
portrait of themselves."[15] Indeed, Glaspell is so modest that she
does not even append that self-portrait. Jelinek also mentions that
nineteenth-century literary women often wrote portraits of male
writers but did not write their own autobiographies.[16] One might
conclude that Glaspell belongs to a long tradition of self-effacing
females, but Bella Brodzki and Celeste Schenck suggest that
women used their status as alien or "other" to experiment in a
positive sense: "Being *between two covers* with somebody else ultimately replaces singularity with alterity in a way that is dramati-
cally female, provides a mode of resisting reification and essential-
ism, and most important, allows for more radical experimentation
in autobiographical form."[17]

In *The Road to the Temple*, Glaspell uses a hybrid form with a
suggestive subtlety in order to satisfy both the patriarchal world
and her own needs. Her ostensible purpose, or "cover," is to valo-
rize Cook as a great man despite his lack of conventional greatness
with the result, as Marcia Noe so wittily observes, that "the effect
is rather like someone standing directly in front of one of the
foothills of the Alps and mistaking it for Mont Blanc."[18] Her con-
cealed motive, to enact the final stages of her mourning for Cook,
is more successfully rendered. Midway through the book she is still
trying to keep him alive for himself and for herself: "There are

moments that remain as pictures, and he who filled those moments is a living person as long as the mind in which they live has life" (194), but she recognizes the increasing difficulty: "one moment there for you, then the darkness and silence that are the miles between" (196). To complete her mourning, Glaspell must come to terms with her role in Cook's life and his role in hers, in other words, to achieve an appraisal sufficiently realistic yet sympathetic, to live without him without dismissing her years with him as some-how mistaken. The mainly chronological structure of *The Road to the Temple* facilitates this task since Glaspell can examine and work through her feelings for Cook at various stages of their rela-tionship, including, curiously enough, what she learns of the years before she met him.

In the first half of *The Road to the Temple*, Glaspell maintains her presence in the narrative despite her literal absence from Cook's life. As she recounts anecdotes of his frontier ancestors, particu-larly Ira and Rachel Cook, she frequently flashes forward to Cook's and her life in Greece. She compares Ira Cook's friendship with his neighbor Morton with the friendship between Jig and shep-herd Elias Scaramouche (7–8), and so implies that she and Cook are also pioneers. In addition, Glaspell uses a kind of hypothetical flash-forward since she presents Cook's talented, original, but thwarted mother, "Ma-Mie," as what Glaspell herself could have been if Ma-Mie had not formed Cook, who would form Glaspell in a more liberated mode: Ma-Mie "was ill-nourished by the life of that place in those days; one feels that a richer personality would have resulted from richer soil—a little too much energy burned up in just keeping alive" (17).

By presenting her romantic predecessors as precursors of herself, Glaspell even manages the difficult task of discussing them without evident jealousy. The young Cook is foolish enough to prefer "the belle of the Tri-Cities" (67), Margery, to poet Elsa, "even though he suspected she had neither the beauty of mind nor the power for love he felt in Elsa" (73), the qualities Cook would prize in Glas-pell. Cook is even jejune enough to believe no great woman can come from a rural, somewhat straitened, background, a notion Glaspell would later disprove. Of his students at the University of Iowa, he writes, "Students poor. . . . Puritanic distrust of pleasure and beauty" (80), and speculates, "What if we could find a woman who could be drawn into this truthful and passionate mental life!" (86). He later thinks he has found one in Vera, but she belies her name by renouncing him because he "is still a married man" (146), as Glaspell ultimately would not.

Glaspell is also present in her account of Cook's early years by her intense sense of their contrasting youths. As Ann Larabee notes, "class and gender distinctions between Glaspell and Cook led to the hierarchical structure of their relationship and perhaps to her uneasy worship of him."[19] Glaspell's admiration for Cook was also tinged with envy, for he was handed opportunities, such as a college education and European travel, that she was compelled to earn for herself and enjoy at a later age. She also covets not only iconoclast Ma-Mie but his more conservative but eminently reliable father, of whom she writes, "few boys have had better fathers" (68). Glaspell's most telling comment is this understatement so typical of her: "George Cram Cook grew up in a town that had a Cook Memorial Library, the Cook Home, and a Cook Memorial Church. I am constrained to say again—there having been no Glaspell Home for the Friendless—these things are relevant" (13).

Glaspell clearly conveys the sense that Cook was so far ahead of her that she feared she would never catch up. When she relishes her image of herself as a rebel, "a little improper" (191), who attends the Monist Club on Sunday morning instead of church, Cook is already there, leading the discussion (191–92, 195). She remembers that she had met Cook earlier when she visited his mother: "She went out and got him. He came reluctantly" (194). Glaspell's sense of unworthiness is reinforced when she sees Renan's *Life of Christ* in his mother's parlor and uses it to try to engage him in conversation.

> I wanted to talk to George Cook. "Oh, you read it in French," I said. "Yes," he replied, a little, it seemed to me, as if it were a strange thing to comment on. I felt foolish and some years later reproached him with not having been nice to me (194).

Glaspell may have seen Cook as her superior in 1907, but years later she has enough self-esteem to reproach him for his earlier snobbery. This anecdote comes about halfway through the book and is a good example of the way Glaspell uses the triple perspective of the distant past, the more recent past, and the present to evaluate her relationship with Cook and her own growth as an independent thinker.

Glaspell's sense of inferiority to Cook reflects, and then is reinforced by, the way his life and ideas permeate her writing. For example, Cook stresses the dangerous but necessary role of the pioneer or the forerunner to the progress of the species, a notion reiterated to tedium in the many and lengthy excerpts from his writings that Glaspell provides. He also emphasizes the importance of mother-love to evolution in comments such as "He saw the age-long war all mothers wage with death" (117). Pioneering and mothering are, as we have seen, central and inextricably linked themes in Glaspell's works. Glaspell also used Cook's ancestors for the Mortons of *Inheritors* and his experiments with a greenhouse and flirtation with madness for *The Verge*, to cite two examples from many. Significantly, in her copious excerpts from his jottings, Glaspell makes no attempt to conceal her sources, as if here too, she is working off her debt to Cook.

A chapter entitled "Our House in Provincetown" is emblematic of the symbiosis of Cook and Glaspell's relationship. Glaspell describes Cook as tearing down walls and deciding on all sorts of new configurations; she appears as an admiring audience who will later put all the improvements to use. When a doctor diagnoses a heart problem in Glaspell, Cook builds her an elevator so that she can "work in an upstairs room, feeling safe then, shut away from the world" (231). She states of the elevator:

> When I go up, pulling ever so gently on the rope, the pipes go down, and with my descent, the pipes rise. For years we have worked together most understandingly. I can walk up the stairs now, but I use the elevator a good deal—so personal an elevator, not attuned to any one else as perfectly as to me (232).

As female, younger, and less privileged, Glaspell required shelter in order to write; at the same time, she needed the experience from which her status barred her in order to feed her writing. Cook provided that refuge and, vicariously, that experience; in her writings, she supplied the tangible fruits of that experience in a way that he could not, so that "for years" they "worked together most understandingly." Again, she multiplies her perspective: the Glaspell who used Cook as an elevator, a wellspring of ideas and incidents, no longer absolutely requires him, but chooses to use her memories of him because, through her life with him and through her writing, she has made them her own.

In *The Road to the Temple*, Glaspell's maternal metaphors function much like the elevator. She refers to Mollie Price as the woman who "became the mother of [Cook's] children" (178–79), a status Glaspell was unable to achieve because of a stillbirth and miscarriages. As in the case of the house and elevator, she eventually triumphs, as Ann Larabee states: "As author, Glaspell played it both ways: she was disciple and mother creator, like the Mary who knelt at Jesus's feet."[20] At the time of her ruined hopes for children, however, Glaspell did not feel particularly triumphant, nor did she find authorship sufficiently compensatory, as the end of "Our House in Provincetown" attests.

> I do not know how to tell the story of Jig without telling this. Women say to one: "You have your work. Your books are your children, aren't they?" And you look at the diapers airing by the fire, and wonder if they really think you are like that. . . .
>
> There were other disappointments, and Jig and I did not have children. Perhaps it is true there was a greater intensity between us because of this. Even that, we would have foregone.
>
> We had Nilla and Harl [Jig and Mollie's] children almost every summer. We would put away bathing-suits and little boats in September, and get them out again in June (239).

The Road to the Temple is dedicated "to Nilla and Harl" as if, though she could not provide their father with children, she would provide the children with inspiring memories of their father, and in that way serve the future for which Cook had such grandiose hopes.

The Road to the Temple exemplifies the reasons Glaspell feels justified in appropriating and transforming Cook's life and ideas. Quite simply, she is much the better writer. The excerpts from Cook's plays, stories, poems, and occasional jottings are soporific. Again and again, they sound a single note: Cook's overweening ambition to become a Nietzschean superman and lead humanity to greater heights. Aspirations may be of some interest, but they cannot sustain that interest without their enactment, successful or otherwise. In contrast, the chapters in which Glaspell writes Cook's story in her own words provide that dramatic element. They are as gripping as good short stories and almost as enthralling as Glaspell's best plays. To cite just one example, in "World of Symbols," the account of Cook's journey to the verge of madness, Glaspell writes about Cook as she would a fictional character in that she employs the third-person limited omniscient point of view, what Henry James called "central consciousness." She describes Cook's internal experience, but in her voice and with her own sense of pacing and structure, as if she cannot bear to waste such excellent material by presenting it through Cook's monotonous jottings.

As the book continues, and Glaspell and the marriage grow older, Cook appears to function less as an inspiration and more as a bully to Glaspell. As she characterizes it, his method is to cast her, if she opposed him, in the role of the spoil-sport, nay-sayer, or incompetent who narrow-mindedly thwarts genius: "An exasperating thing about him was that his enthusiasms often deprived you of your most righteous resentments" (316). His demand that she write a play for his new stage may have resulted in that delicately-crafted gem, *Trifles*, but other commands detracted from her writing time, for example, when Cook invented a new process for molding figures for a sun-dial.

> I was the assistant. It was my business to have more plaster right there, the water at just such a temperature, and to pour at precisely the right tempo at the exact moment or—"God damn it, it's ruined!" At first I was hurt by profanity; had I not been getting the things ready for hours? Had I not done my best? Could angels ask more? Yes, indeed they could, and did. I do not know just what went on in the house of Benvenuto Cellini, but in our locked house you had the feeling death would be done for a slip of the arm. And why not? Was not this the work into which the moods of the days had gone? Were not these the figures to support the sundial, and symbols of our relation to truth beyond our world? (280–81).

The comparison to Cellini and the rhetorical questions about the overriding importance of art do not succeed in distracting the reader from Cook's monomania and his disregard for Glaspell's feelings. Again, part of the problem is the fact that Cook was no

Cellini, and, to paraphrase Noe, we have the uncomfortable feeling that one of the Alps is bowing down before a foothill.

Cook apparently could not deal with an adult and successful Glaspell who was no longer an uncritical hero-worshipper. One might even speculate that the move to Greece was partially motivated by the desire to remove Glaspell from her eminence and put himself back in charge as her mentor and guide, the one who could speak the language. Neither could he accept a woman who was no longer a source of sexual excitement to him, though the problem could as easily be attributed to Cook's age, drinking, and health, as to Glaspell's waning bodily charms.

> "I do not want to live beyond sex," Jig said to me. One night, unable to sleep, feeling alone, not enough loved, he came into my hut [at Kalania], sat on the boughs beside me. I cannot tell how things were with him, without saying something of this. He was unhappy because it was not as it had been in the first years. . . . Was not that one of the things we had to accept, I said. After years together, something goes, yet is it all loss? Does not something also come? He did not care for that way of looking at it, he said. He was the lover. . . . Yet I think he knew I always loved him (388–89).

Glaspell expresses sympathy for Cook and his ideal, but she arranges the scene so that she gets the last word and displays the greater wisdom; he seems fixated in adolescence while she has grown to know what love truly is.

Glaspell foreshadows the consequences of asserting her own will in opposition to that of Cook when she tells of Ma-Mie's desire that Jig take a noncombatant's job in support of the Allies during the First World War. "He replied scornfully to this suggestion, and she in turn wrote unsympathetically of his feeling" (300). Unfortunately, the quarrel was not resolved before his mother's death, and "Jig wished he might have seen her once more, told her more patiently what it was he felt" (300). Patience, however, was a virtue of which Cook was increasingly incapable as he felt the years go by without his mystic fulfillment. He projected his sense of failure onto Glaspell. At Kalania, Cook had a wild bird that he had tamed enough to eat crumbs from his hand. When he one day threw a piece of bread at the bird, Glaspell remonstrated with him, with these consequences: "I could not believe it was happening when Jig seized my arm and I looked up into the blaze of rage, of hate, it seemed, in his eyes. . . . There was a moment when I was afraid" (397–98). He was furious at Glaspell because she had not trusted him enough to perceive that this was part of his training program for the bird. He could no longer train Glaspell.

As Cook withdrew further into his obsessions, Glaspell made some gestures of self-assertion that would insure her psychological survival. When he wanted to found a Delphic Players, she told him that she was "through with groups" (403). Her resistance to the turmoil of his constant attempts to re-make their lives through drinking, partying, and new projects is evident in this rare vignette of the ordered household she wished to maintain. "To-Puppy would be sleeping on his own little bed, Nilla in her room working at Greek, and Jig at his big table, books and papers around him. I liked the feeling that my household was safe; that they were doing the things it seemed their part to do" (420).

With her typical optimism, Glaspell tries to salvage success from the debacle of their life in Greece by depicting a moment of reconciliation before Cook's final illness.

> This night Jig and I could talk. It was as if we were lovers who had been long separated, though it was of experiences shared we talked. We talked of what it was we had wanted from life; of greater success we might have had, but of a searching, an asking, we had shared. We saw one another, and with tenderness (431).

This moment is undercut by one seven pages later in which a terrified Glaspell cannot move the desperately ill Cook to better medical care because of the inclement winter weather. "I would put more logs on the fire and sit by it, hearing Jig talk [in delirium], now in ancient Greek, now in the modern language. I would think of many things. I wished we were in a hospital in Athens" (438). Their communion at Kalania was momentary and possibly illusory. The status quo has reasserted itself: she is responsible for a man who cannot recognize or speak to her as an autonomous individual in her own right and in her own language.

Despite Glaspell's many kind words about Cook, the reader cannot be fully distracted from the misery she often felt in Delphi. By the time of his death, the reader's sadness over the tragedy is mingled with a sense of relief that Glaspell is free of her burden. On the last page, about his burial at Delphi according to Greek rites she comments: "Our parting, a personal grief, became almost an intrusion. He had been taken into the great past he loved and realized" (445). Glaspell seems to be taking the high road here, looking at the wider perspective, but she is implying that he loved his idea of Greece more than he loved her.

Glaspell ends *The Road to the Temple* with one of Cook's poems; she gives him the last word, perhaps as if presenting the whole book to him as a gift, the way a mother presents a newborn to a father. But perhaps not. Glaspell may have learned through her bitter trials in Greece and her terrible solitude after Cook's death that one cannot live someone else's dream; she gives him back his life with his words because she needs to reclaim her own.

6

Ghostly Revenants and Symbolic Sons: Fugitives Return

When Susan Glaspell returned from Greece after Cook's death early in 1924, she found a milieu quite different from the one she had left two years before. Not only had the Provincetown Players become more commercialized, but also much of the avant garde had dissipated into factionalism or frivolity, including the women's movement.[1] Glaspell may have felt like a female Rip Van Winkle, but one who found that society had regressed instead of progressed, or perhaps like a wandering spirit without the ballast of mate or movement. She tried to replace what she had lost through living with Norman Matson, a younger and much less successful writer whose career she tried to promote; in many ways he became a son as well as a lover.

Glaspell's disorientation in the face of her changed world and changed life is manifested in her three major works of the end of the decade: two novels, *Brook Evans* (1928) and *Fugitive's Return* (1929), and her final produced play, the Pulitzer Prize-winning *Alison's House* (1930). The three works have female protagonists who are not literally ghosts but who reproach and admonish the present with the specter of their tragically thwarted lives. Naomi Kellogg Evans of *Brook Evans* is a living ghost in two of that novel's five books and dead in two others, but her legacy remains alive to her family for two generations. In *Fugitive's Return*, Irma Lee Shraeder is literally alive throughout the novel, but she is mute and spectral for much of the action. The title character of *Alison's House* is long dead, but her actions and wishes haunt her descendants and admirers.

In the introduction to *Haunting the House of Fiction: Feminist Perspectives on Ghost Stories*, Lynette Carpenter and Wendy K. Kolmar cite a number of characteristics of such tales, many of them shared by Glaspell's work at the end of the twenties, such as the "empowerment of the powerless by death" and the depiction of the "natural and supernatural experience along a continuum." As Glaspell's title indicates, Alison's is one of the "houses haunted by women" that "provide a powerful image of the house as an embodiment of female tradition." Finally, all three of Glaspell's works use ghostly women to "critique mainstream male culture, values, and tradition."[2] Glaspell's works differ from those described by Carpenter and Kolmar in that Glaspell seems too despondent over the plight of women to place her hopes in younger women but instead turns to unusually sensitive males who serve as symbolic sons.

Brook Evans dramatizes the ways in which the sins of the fathers, abetted by the mothers, afflict the children, who, in turn, pass the legacy of misunderstandings and broken dreams to the next generation, until the chain is broken by a remarkably empathetic young man. As this description indicates, *Brook Evans* is a highly schematic novel.

Book I is set in the Midwest of 1888. Like Romeo and Juliet, Naomi Kellogg and Joe Copeland carry on a clandestine affair despite the opposition of their families. The brook that divides their farms is the meeting place that unites the two lovers and serves as a symbol of love as the life-force throughout the novel. After Joe is accidentally killed by farm machinery, Naomi learns that she is pregnant. Naomi can anticipate her father's response by remembering his treatment of a runaway horse: "Oh, she could not believe it . . . that it was her father who jumped up and down and lashed his horse like that."[3] Mr. Kellogg's possessive and patriarchal wrath is supported by his religion: he was "fervent in everything having to do with the Bible and church" (23).

Adrienne Rich writes that "patriarchy depends on the mother to act as a conservative influence, imprinting future adults with patriarchal values," as Joe and Naomi's mothers so aptly illustrate.[4]

Mrs. Copeland "thinks she's better than other folks" (10); she is male-identified and takes her status from the Copeland name. When Naomi informs her of her pregnancy in the hope that she would be delighted to have something left of Joe, Mrs. Copeland cries, "Glad to know my son deceived me and left a bastard to besmirch our name!" (34). She is so protective of patrilineage that she even questions the child's paternity: "How's there any telling — with loose women like you?" (34).

Mrs. Kellogg is not so much male-identified as browbeaten. One of her first statements indicates how well she had learned her ineffectuality: "'Oh well,' said Mrs. Kellogg, helplessly; she had a way of saying 'Oh — well,' either before jelly which would not jell or before other manifestations of life she could not control" (9). Naomi only remembers one occasion when she refused her father; as a small child she heard her mother's "*No*" (47) from her parents' bedroom, an early lesson in sexual politics. Mrs. Kellogg's customary timidity is linked to her version of an angry patriarchal god, society: "She had no courage when it came to what people would say" (46).

Mrs. Kellogg teaches Naomi what she considers the feminine survival skills of mendacity, self-sacrifice, and guilt. Her mother tells Naomi that her Uriah Heep-like suitor Caleb Evans is "'such a good man' . . . and when her mother took that tone it seemed a little insincere" (13). She advises Naomi to marry Caleb, who is willing to have her despite the pregnancy, because "sometimes we have to force ourselves to do things" (29). Daughterly guilt is her ultimate weapon. When proud Mr. Kellogg's rage at Naomi's visit to Mrs. Copeland is exacerbated by her mother's copious tears, he exclaims to Naomi, "You see, do you? See what you've done to the mother that loved you and worked for you?" (39).

Naomi is mastered by the law of the fathers as transmitted by the mothers. She marries Caleb Evans and moves with him to Colorado where Book II begins in 1907 when Joe and Naomi's daughter Brook Evans is eighteen, about the same age as her mother at the time of her pregnancy. Brook is the Jamesian central consciousness of this book and through her we see how the ancestral legacy has pursued the family even into the New World of the West.

Years ago Caleb lost his own chance to found a line when his five-year-old son by Naomi, John, was killed by stampeding cattle. He seems fond of Brook, but uses her to keep Naomi mindful of her sin and his "charity" and authority. Brook remembers that when her mother wanted a room built for Brook, "there had been a good deal of trouble about that, whereas things Brook asked herself, if they did not involve father's principles, he was more than likely to do for her" (64). Even when his "principles" are at stake, Naomi is the one he wants to oppose. When Caleb does not want Brook to attend a party with Tony Ross because he is Italian, Native American, and Catholic, "it was not to her, it was to her mother, he kept saying no" (91).

Like *Fidelity's* adulterous Ruth Holland, Naomi sees herself as serving her sentence in the prison of the mountains, which "shut me in" (66). Like another adulteress, Hester Prynne in *The Scarlet Letter*, she expresses herself through affection for her daughter. She saves culinary treats for Brook and even takes money out of Caleb's pocketbook for her (72–73). Indeed, she attempts to live vicariously through Brook; the room she had Caleb build for Brook was modeled on the room at her parents' house from which she stole to meet Joe. Brook is not grateful for her mother's intense interest in her life; predictably, she responds to it as an overwhelming burden. At one point, she wants to hug her mother but refrains: "Somehow, it wasn't natural to do it, though she half knew her mother was starving for it. Perhaps that was why she couldn't" (72).

Because she cannot understand her mother's motivations, Brook craves what she perceives as normal, ironically, the very patriarchal values that made her mother the woman she is. Like her stepfather and her maternal grandfather, she values churchgoing because "she had a sense of being part of things as they should be, of being taken in where she was one with others" (77). Since she does not know why her mother avoids church, dresses poorly in order to spend money on Brook, and maintains her isolation from society, Brook wants a mother who is a dutiful handmaiden of imperialism like the pious missionary Mrs. Waite (59). When Naomi reveals her past to Brook in order to gain her sympathy and affection, Brook is so naively narrow-minded that she "felt embarrassed. It was as if mother had taken off too many of her clothes" (103). "It was right a father should be strict" (104), Brook concludes.

The consequences of this tragedy of intergenerational errors are demonstrated in Book III. With Naomi as the central consciousness we learn that Joe's death, her illegitimate pregnancy, and her rejection and exile by her parents are not the only causes of her desperation. Caleb has been another source of misery, especially in the marriage bed, a scene of what is essentially rape. "She could have come to feel friendly, loyal, perhaps something like affectionate toward him, had it not been for those violations at night. . . . He must know that she submitted with loathing" (131). After their son John's death, Caleb, who had some such problems before, becomes completely impotent, but Naomi's relief provides another source for Caleb's peevish animosity.

Naomi copes with her suffering by believing that, Christ-like, she can use it to atone for the transgressions of others, in this case, for what she hopes will be a successful romance between Brook and Tony. She imagines telling Brook, "Oh, don't worry! I have paid a price. I have paid your way!" (111). She evades the fate of *Trifle*'s Minnie Wright when she stops herself from stabbing Caleb in his sleep and decides to tell Tony of Brook's true parentage so that he might pursue his courtship with her support and despite Caleb's opposition. Unbeknown to Brook, Naomi even forwards their elopement, but on the night of their flight Brook learns that her mother has told Tony her secret, so she cuts off her nose to spite her face by again rebelling against her mother's desires. She leaves Tony in the lurch and runs off to join Mrs. Waite in the mission fields. Brook even lies to justify herself, to vilify her mother and Tony, and to augment her mother's sufferings when she claims in a letter to her father that Tony tried to seduce her with Naomi's connivance.

Book IV is set about twenty years later. Brook is thirty-eight, her mother's age when Brook left Colorado, and Brook's son, Evans Leonard, is eighteen, Brook's age at that time. She recognizes that Mrs. Waite pushed her into a safe marriage with the older, chronically ill Captain Leonard, whom Brook regarded with affection but not passion. Like her mother, she has rebelled against church and family ties, and now decides not to repeat her marital mistake with Colonel Fowles, an older, conservative, friend of her late husband. At last she can perceive her mother's situation with wisdom derived from experience.

There had been nothing in her own life that would have gone on living through twenty barren years. Mother had known only a few months of love — then loss, shame, and oh, loneliness — long, relentless. But there was a light that never went out. It burned in tragic beauty until — until I put out all the light of her spirit, thought Brook (208).

Brook is still quite limited spiritually, but she resolves to make up for lost time.

Glaspell presents Brook with the means of change, a young and passionate Icelandic mathematician, Erik Helge. He is based on Norman Matson, to whom the novel is dedicated, with some elements of George Cram Cook added, such as his firing as a "dangerous teacher" (191).[5] In some ways Helge is a fantasy figure since he seems such a perfect spiritual as well as physical match: "To another it might seem strange how much of their talk had been of impersonal things, though none of it seemed impersonal, charged with an intimacy curiously profound" (226). He claims that he will "rescue" her "from all that is not life" (248), but he crashes their car into a tree. They are uninjured, but his intense sensation-seeking is a form of selfishness since he wants Brook immediately to accompany him to China rather than visit the dying Caleb Evans, who has moved back to Naomi's old Midwestern home. Glaspell again shows how a maternal legacy becomes warped in transmission: Brook decides to go with Helge, to follow love, but in order to do so she avoids a direct confrontation with her American past and instead sends her son Evans as her substitute.

Evans is a rather androgynous character since he is portrayed with conventionally masculine strength and reticence, but he has Naomi's eyes (188) and seems almost preternaturally empathetic, a "boy who understood so many things it would not seem his years had had time to teach him" (183). If Helge is the fantasy lover, Evans is certainly the ideal son. Brook sends him to the Midwest without telling him either her own or Naomi's story because she recalled the way her mother's tale "had repelled her" (256), and she fears his response to the news of her impending union with Helge. As Judith Arcana writes of the mothers of sons, "We are hesitant to make too big an impact, or to be too visible in our sons' lives — at the same time that we are desperate to do so, longing to build bridges between ourselves and our male children."[6]

Here Brook's fears are also part of her reaction against her mother's course of action, telling the truth, but Brook's maternal decision works for the best because her child is male and is not culturally conditioned to an exclusive focus on emotions and courtship and so can take a broader, and hence more sympathetic, view. Book V could be entitled "Cultured Expatriate Meets the Babbitts" as Evans Leonard encounters the vulgarly materialistic latter-day Kelloggs. Evans, however, manages to maintain his gentlemanly demeanor: he tolerates his kin and understands his mother's decision to marry Helge, possibly because of the mystic influences of heredity, or Naomi's photograph, which showed one who "saw, felt things" (278), or even the "intimations from the brook" (288). Or perhaps just because Evans is a man for whom "life was adventure" (287); he can act for himself rather than react defensively to the actions of others, as had Naomi and Brook. For Naomi, he would have been the perfect progeny in a sexist world; her vicarious participation would have been tempered by the gender difference, and that difference would also allow his actions to be autonomous and triumphant in contrast to Brook's pathetic rebellions against her mother. At the end of the 1920s, Glaspell seems to suggest that only men can reap the benefits of androgyny.

In *Brook Evans*, Naomi's ghostly legacy influences two generations in a highly schematic and chronological presentation. In contrast, the "ghost" of *Fugitive's Return* is present throughout the action, and the time scheme is broken to show how she arrived at that spectral state and then how she returns to the living. At the beginning of the novel, Irma Lee Shraeder is bereft of her identity since she no longer can define herself through others. Her husband left her three years ago and her small daughter recently died of infantile paralysis. Irma plans to complete her self-erasure by killing herself. She is interrupted by her cousin Janet who gives her a new identity and destination in the form of the passport and boat tickets of one Myra Freeman who cannot make the trip to Greece. This is not a real transformation since, if one changes "y" for "i," Myra is an anagram of Irma; the surname is "Free-man," as if that is her new job, instead of being a "Freewoman." As her double name suggests, Irma is a ghost hovering between two worlds, at home in neither, until she finds her symbolic son and erstwhile lover.

Glaspell's remarkable attunement to women's patterns of growth make *Fugitive's Return* an almost uncanny enactment of the stages presented in Carol Gilligan's groundbreaking *In a Different Voice: Psychological Theory and Women's Development*. At the beginning of the novel, Irma is in the first phase with "an initial focus on caring for the self in order to ensure survival."[7] Like a wounded animal, Irma withdraws from others, even to the point of becoming mute. On the ship to Greece, she is observed by the married Allie Mayer and her unrequited lover and chivalrous gallant of nine years, the appropriately named John Knight. He refers to Irma as "a ghost," and she does indeed appear to have ghostly powers:

> She herself was in the nothingness — so they [her fellow passengers] did not get to her. They could not touch her with their disturbances, their worries, ambitions, disappointments, happinesses. And yet, because they could not touch her, because nothing from her came back, she could see them, know about them, as she had never done when herself disturbed. Almost without looking at them, she knew about them.[8]

Like a ghost, she feels transparent. "Now that there was nothing within herself to impede, congest, feeling that came from others formed itself into speculation, thin, clear, unimportant" (37).

Two years later Irma-Myra is living at Delphi like a visiting ghost or like a goddess sojourning among mortals. She has "the only house within the sacred precinct" (49) and is known to the villagers as the Kyria of the Archai. One mother tells her child that "the Kyria was the prophetess of the temple, and that she did not speak because the temple had fallen" (51). Again, Irma has a new identity, but it is another way of avoiding coming to terms with her true self based on her past.

In some ways, Irma's ghostly status allows her to learn about her fellow women in a way that her previous focus on her personal tragedies had not. She had always felt something of a freak as a woman, "that she had moved just outside a rhythm in which others moved facilely" (3), but when placed unequivocally on the outside as a mute foreigner, she can perceive that her problems are those of all women. She may be in Greece, where the topography and language are different, but the oppressive patriarchy remains the same.

Four women exhibit aspects of Irma's past and the roles of all women. Vascelo is a widow, who, because of her two children, knows that she will be unable to get a new husband. She is jealous of other women and so, like Naomi of *Brook Evans*, directs toward her daughter "a passion at times too heavy-laden with feeling that should have gone elsewhere" (75). The second woman, Theodora, like Irma, is a refugee, in her case from the war in Turkey, but unlike Irma, she is "the artist" (73) who can pour out her passions in song and dance. Unfortunately, her tragic experiences in her homeland and her artistic ability do not make her more human or sympathetic, but less so. She seems to want to inflict on other women some of what she has herself suffered and does so with the traditional woman's weapon of her tongue, as when she mercilessly teases Vascelo.

Stamula presents a largely happy image of traditional domesticity in that she participates in a woman's culture, particularly in weaving, which she teaches Irma. In this sense, she is the woman whom Irma thought she should be in her marriage to Dan Shraeder. Stamula and Irma seem to replace the patriarchal culture of Apollo with an older maternal order when on "the stage of the old theater . . . the two women wove" (54). There they return to the origins of the thespian art because of their differing languages and Irma's muteness.

> Stamula would act a little play of her husband cross because she
> was late, herself placating him, and hurrying to put dishes upon
> the table, until finally he was seated before his food, sulky, but
> eating voraciously (65).

Although these playlets eventually make "the Kyria laugh" (66), it is the shared laughter of the oppressed, which provides a safe outlet for rebellion through mockery of the masters.

The shepherd girl Constantina, though, is really Irma's spiritual self-image or self-parody in that she is an extreme victim of patriarchal expectations. Her father is disgusted with her because she is his fourth daughter and he desires "a child that will make a man" (59). Her appearance bars her from serving as a sex or status object since "she was little more than a dwarf, so dry and wizened she looked as much an old woman as a girl" (60–61). Constantina is raped by Andreas in order to make her respect his precedence as a male shepherd. He declares he would prefer going to jail to marrying her, and so, for the village, "this settled it. No one would marry her now. She was not a woman. She was a shepherd" (63).

As Irma witnesses these women and their roles in their male-dominated society, she begins to move toward Gilligan's second step, in which "the good is equated with caring for others."[9] As is so typical of Glaspell, a dog is the symbol of the world's suffering. Irma saves a stray dog from hanging by a mob of villagers by breaking her silence and asking, "Was it for this Jesus died?" (89). As if a specter had spoken, the hanging halts. For Irma, this is only a tentative step because she cannot really move into an ethic of care until she confronts her past and, in effect, cares for her former self, which she does in an extended flashback that comprises the middle third of *Fugitive's Return*.

Like the problems of the women in *Brook Evans*, Irma's trials are the result of paternal failures abetted by maternal repression. The Lees had once owned most of the west side of town, but only the land around the homestead remained theirs. Irma's father was a foreman over day laborers and her mother, like Mrs. Kellogg, a well-intentioned but ineffectual housekeeper. If Irma had not known any other life, she might have simply accepted her lot as it was, but her mother had known a better life, the one lived by her sister, and she wants Irma to experience it by trying to keep up with her wealthy cousin Janet and her crowd. These attempts were doomed to failure, for, aside from Janet, these girls were snobs more interested in the fact that Irma lacked an indoor toilet than that Irma lacked self-confidence. Glaspell is not indicting Irma for acquiescing to superficial values, but is demonstrating how hard it is to form a self from an impoverished life outside a social order. Of Irma's longing for Janet's way of life, Glaspell writes, "she wanted these things in common, and in the security of them she could more freely have been herself" (113).

As her family's economic and social status continued to decline, Irma was faced with a choice. She was much attracted to Horace, a young farmer "who was unlike any one she had known, and Irma came to the conclusion the difference was in his acting upon what went on within him" (135). On the other hand, she also knew that her mother's "greatest fear, her torment" was "that the daughter she idolized, for whom she would have worked to the death, might be sucked into a life from which she could not escape" (139). As in *Brook Evans*, overly intense maternal aspirations backfired, and Irma eventually married Dan Shraeder, an architect and party-lover, despite the fact that she realized that "her love for Horace opened her to it all, and her love for Dan enclosed her with itself" (164). A caged, limited woman is not good company, and Irma gradually alienated Dan by her inability to let herself go and respond to him, either by participating in his life or letting him into hers, particularly sexually.

Instead, Irma constructed two defenses against life. The first was the remodeling and tending of her house on Cape Cod, which became a replica of the fortress of her personality, serving to repel others, including Dan, whose work was in Boston. Part of her attraction to the house was that she identified it with her paternal ancestors who came to the Midwest from Cape Cod. As she "restored her vineyard," she mused,

> In this older past, this longer rhythm, that which was immediately behind her was somehow less close. Things farther back took to themselves the reality, until she was in a long sweep in which the closest was blurred, as one may look over a thing at hand to that which has distance for perspective (171).

This ancestor worship was, of course, a way of avoiding, keeping "blurred," a true "perspective" on herself.

Like the mothers in *Brook Evans*, Irma tried to erect her second wall against life through her daughter Birdie, though, like Claire Archer in *The Verge*, she had wanted a son because "life seemed too complex for a girl; it seemed her own difficulties would be more likely to reappear in the life of a daughter, and that a son might free himself of them" (174). Had Birdie survived, the pressure of her mother's hopes might have caused "difficulties" enough since Irma, like Naomi Kellogg, was refusing her daughter her individuality, her self, by believing that "in seeing pleasures, opportunities, come to her little girl, it would be as if she herself had had them when she had not had them" (191). Irma was also denying herself by attempting to rewrite the past that was part of her.

Unlike Naomi, Irma is forced to confront her own life because Birdie's death forecloses the possibility of a vicarious life.

At Delphi, as she reviews her past after the incident with the dog, Irma becomes ready to care for others, Gilligan's second stage. She becomes the lover of John Knight, the writer whom she had met on the boat to Greece two years earlier. After making love in a vineyard, he does not become her knight, as he was Allie Mayer's, but asks Irma, "If you are strong enough to be—my great understanding mother, as well as—as well as— . . . my lover" (286), and she consents. As in her vineyard at Cape Cod, she is playing a role written by someone else, though at least Knight is closer to her than her paternal ancestors. Further, in John Knight, she finds the son whom she never had, but either because she is now more mature, or because he is a male, she does not smother him with maternal solicitude the way she did Birdie, but allows him to grow. She recognizes that he remains obsessed with Allie Mayer, but she is not devastated. She can "leave him what he was, loving him for it, even though it withheld from her, and dwelling with him where it was hers to dwell" (294).

In her second consciously chosen act of caring, she demonstrates that she does not need a Knight, for she can rescue herself through rescuing Constantina, who has killed her rapist. Irma's motivation is again maternal feeling: "She is a child, and I promised to help her" (309). As in *Trifles*, two women must secretly save the "murderess" since "there was no punishment too great for a woman who killed a man in Greece" (299). She and Stamula decide to accompany Constantina over the mountain, where Irma and Constantina will begin their journey to the United States. Irma declares to Stamula, "You are my sister," and they part "nodding, as in pledge—the love, understanding, loyalty, that can be between women" (322).

The novel does not end on this note of sisterhood, but with another image of that highly ambiguous vineyard, first related to Irma's paternal ancestors and then to John Knight's need for a lover who is also his "great understanding mother." Irma resolves to make a refuge for Constantina "and into this a tired man might one day walk, a seeker, drawn by the truth of it, needing her" (324). The last lines of the novel are: "She would labor in her vineyard. In her own vineyard would she labor" (324). Irma may be in the process of resolving what Gilligan calls "the confusion between self-sacrifice and care," and approaching a third stage, which promotes more mutually caring relationships.[10] In that case, Irma would provide a refuge for others while nurturing herself on her own terms and turf, "in her own vineyard." The final word of *Fugitive's Return*, "labor," suggests a nonbiological form of motherhood that will nurture the self along with the evolution of humanity, a hope frequently sounded in Glaspell's plays. This hope, though, is a limited one in *Fugitive's Return*, for the symbolic son, John Knight, will remain the active wanderer and seeker while Constantina and Irma, the ghostly revenants or weird sisters, tend the vineyard at home.

In her play *Alison's House*, Glaspell presents a ghostly revenant whose piquant personality and famous poems haunt her family and admirers eighteen years after her death. Alison Stanhope is based on Emily Dickinson, but the poet's family would not allow Glaspell to use the Dickinson name or quote from her poems.[11] Even so, Alison is characterized by many of the traits we readily associate with Dickinson: a white dress (124); sherry-colored eyes (147); a love of Emerson's poetry (97); a non-literary sister as devoted watchdog; and a rebellion against the conception of God as a stern and unloving patriarch (103).[12] Through the play, Glaspell evaluates the consequences of one aspect of Dickinson's life, her unconsummated love for a married man, here rendered as Alison Stanhope's renunciation of a married Harvard professor in answer to the pleas of her scandal-fearing brother (140–41).

A cheerful and uplifting reading of the play would stress that by renouncing an earthly lover and biological children, Alison could become the perfect mother through nurturing her symbolic children, nephew Eben and niece Elsa, and through her poems that sustain other women, her spiritual daughters. Unlike an often harassed biological mother, Aunt Alison has the time and energy to manifest "playfulness" (92) toward Eben and Elsa by presenting them with charmingly quaint gifts like "pebbles from the river" (36). Since she is not required to raise them and be their daily disciplinarian, she can side with them against authority. When they disobey, she says, "Alison knows" and "Alison won't tell" (36). Her use of the third-person sounds at once childlike and godlike, as does her more consolatory, "Come to Alison. . . . Alison will make it right" (113). Eben even trusts her enough to show her his youthful attempts at poetry. In other words, Alison seems like the perfect mother, sufficiently powerful to assist, but still enough of a child to understand.

In accordance with such an optimistic reading of the play, to the women of the future Alison's nurturing legacy is her recently discovered love poetry. These verses express for other women what they are incapable of articulating for themselves. In the catharsis that Alison provides for them, they can find succor and solace. As Ann, a young woman newly in love, declares, "Alison said it — for women" (150), and so once again Alison proves herself the ideal mother-figure.

The play, however, is much more ambiguous than this emphasis on Glaspell's typical themes indicates.[13] The first, and, until Alison, the only woman artist-protagonist in Glaspell's plays and novels, is Ernestine Hubers of her first novel, *The Glory of the Conquered* (1909). Ernestine did manage to have it all, albeit sequentially, as she achieved artistic mastery despite and because of submerging her career in that of her husband. Sandra M. Gilbert and Susan Gubar find this absence of women artist-figures typical of women writers of Glaspell's era: they face their fears of a woman's life without art "by imagining characters who are unable to achieve the aesthetic release their authors themselves attain by the very creation of these figures."[14] When Glaspell creates her second major artist, twenty years after the first, she returns to the late nineteenth-century notion that a woman can either be an artist or a mate, not both.

Glaspell, however, is presenting a devastating critique of these rigidly defined, mutually exclusive roles for women. Alison's legacy, the life and art of renunciation, is not an unmixed blessing. Her sister Agatha is so obsessively jealous a caretaker that she will not even reveal what kind of pen Alison used (27). Agatha is another example of Glaspell's strong sense of the evils of living vicariously; had Alison run away with her lover, Agatha might have been compelled to live her own life. Another victim is Alison's brother Stanhope who remained in an unhappy marriage, despite his love for another woman, out of a foolish consistency; he chooses to suffer as he compelled Alison to do.

The younger generation also has lost at least as much as they have gained from Alison's legacy. Her nephew Eben, following the renunciatory pattern set by his aunt, is trapped in a marriage to Laura, a woman as rigidly conventional as the Laura of *Bernice*, and so he is unable to write poetry (74). (One might also speculate that he suffers from the anxiety of influence in regard to his famous aunt.) Alison's niece Elsa follows the example of Alison's spirit, not her actions, by living with a married man, but, like *Fidelity*'s Ruth Holland, finds that sin can be as mundane as virtue, remarking that "Love doesn't have to clothe itself" (115). Alison's much younger nephew Ted, born after her death, sees her legacy as ripe for exploitation: he anticipates great profits from the publication of her love poetry, and, more immediately, to gain better grades on his English themes by telling his professor private details about Alison. Alison's biological descendants are unhappy whether they renounce love for duty like Agatha, Stanhope, and Eben, endure scandal for love like Elsa, or are oblivious to everything but gain like Ted.

Because Alison's descendants are not artists, they are unable to transcend the banalities of their chosen lives. She does, however, have a spiritual heir, another of Glaspell's symbolic sons, the aspiring poet Richard Knowles, who is sent to the Stanhope mansion by his newspaper to cover its sale and the dispersal of the family and Alison's personal effects. There he meets and falls in love with Stanhope's secretary Ann, who loves poetry but cannot write it, and tells Knowles, "I wish I could. . . . That's why I'm so grateful to Alison" (6). Knowles has been walking by the river, as was Alison's custom, and proposes that Ann join him. He tells her that as he walked,

> it was as if [Alison's] thoughts were there. They must have been hers — for they were better than mine. And it seemed to me if you would walk there with me — you and I together — well, that she wouldn't be gone. (96)

Knowles, the symbolic son, can have it all, the poetic legacy of his ghostly mother Alison and the quotidian love of his earthly muse Ann.

Alison's House is an appropriate conclusion for Glaspell's works of the 1920s, for the play's action occurs during the dismantling of Alison's house, as if to suggest that her experience as woman and artist, however painful and limited, can find no place in the modern world. The new house of art will actually be the old dwelling, slightly remodeled, that we readily recognize as the traditional prerogative of the male artist with his ever-subservient female muse. The only gleam of light in these works of the late twenties is that in Richard Knowles, Evans Leonard, and John Knight, Glaspell seems to be anticipating a new, more sensitive, more androgynous kind of man. Sadly, she is bidding farewell to her hopes for her symbolic daughters since they seem bound to the eternal wheel of following or reacting against the warped and warping legacies of their ghostly mothers.

7

Symbolic Fathers and the Revenge of the Dutiful Daughters

In Glaspell's two novels of the 1930s, *Ambrose Holt and Family* (1931) and *The Morning Is Near Us* (1939), sons remain important as a woman's only viable means for a better future in a world that denies her potential. The mother herself, however, is formed by her father in accordance with the desires of patriarchy, as Maggie Lane observes in *Literary Daughters*: "In reacting to whatever attitudes and expectations he brought to the relationship, she made her first negotiation with male power. His approval or disapproval, encouragement or discouragement, pride or disappointment, mattered vitally to her, not only on a personal level but in determining the place she claimed for herself in the world."[1] In Glaspell's novels, as we have seen, a woman's identity is also established in a negative sense by the weak or remote figure of her mother. In order to become the right kind of mother, one who can raise sensitive and strong sons, Glaspell's heroines of the 1930s, Blossom Holt and Lydia Chippman, must evaluate and rewrite the scripts that they have inherited from their parents and break the pattern of women's thwarted lives. They can no longer be dutiful daughters to a warped and warping patriarchal past, so they must make the attempt, so often to their own detriment, to become empowering mothers for the future.

Ambrose Holt and Family is a significantly different version of the story Glaspell told in her last play for the Provincetown Players, *Chains of Dew* (1922). In that play, as Marcia Noe explains, Seymour Standish is a writer who needs to believe that his wife Dottie "is a shallow, silly woman because his ego demands that he feel he is her superior"; at the end of the play, Dottie resolves to let him think so.[2] Glaspell's experiences of the 1920s, particularly catering to George Cram Cook in Greece and Norman Matson in Provincetown, changed her focus from the male writer to the woman who must cope with him. *Ambrose Holt and Family* is the story of Harriette "Blossom" Holt who, at the age of thirty, must learn to renegotiate her relationships with her pampered poet-husband and tyrannical father.

The novel opens with Blossom surveying her garden with the despondent thought that it is not really her garden at all since her mother insists on sending her father's gardener as well as bulbs and plants. What she wants is "her own garden" where she can "experiment, just for fun, to see what would happen."[3] In her desire for self-expression through plants, she resembles Claire Archer in *The Verge*, but, unlike Claire, she is sensitive to the feelings of others and does not take her experiments to their logical, and radical, conclusions: "Though you wanted to have a garden all your own, your parents sent a gardener; and sometimes you wearied, and accepted with thanks" (3). As her name suggests, she identifies herself with that garden and is seeking a means of expression: she want to "have confidence to say what she thought," but "somehow, she hadn't the authority" (6). Blossom wants autonomy, or what Carolyn G. Heilbrun defines as power, "the ability to take one's place in whatever discourse is essential to action and the right to have one's part matter."[4]

Blossom's name is also a vexed issue with her husband, the modernist poet Lincoln Holt who "seemed to want to know her only as Blossom" (8), not Harriette, which she regards as the name of an adult and his equal. When she wishes to discuss his poetry with him, Blossom observes with chagrin that "he said, — run along and play, or what amounted to that. It even seemed that he did not want her to understand it" (9). Like his prototype in *Chains of Dew*, Lincoln wants Blossom in the subservient position of priestess at the shrine of his mysteries.

Through her characterization of Lincoln and his poetry, Glaspell is indicting the increasingly entrenched male modernism that was in the process of excluding her work from the literary canon. Like T. S. Eliot, Lincoln writes of wastelands, "a dump of old cars, a ravine filled with them, heaped crazily one on the other" (27). Like Wallace Stevens, he insists on working a full day in the business world and writing poetry in his spare time. What Glaspell is criticizing here is neither the subject nor the work ethic, but the tendency to exclude others, and so elevate the mysterious, godlike author. In accordance with canonical male modernism, Lincoln's poetry is obscure; his own mother, an intelligent and well-read woman, believes that he should "simplify" (76) it. A prominent critic complains that if Lincoln "were this much, he ought to be more" (19). His inability to communicate with others is actually a fear of exposure, of being found wanting or impotent, and is symbolized by his hidden workroom, which, as Arthur E. Waterman observes, is "neither in nor out of this world, . . . suspended half-way between floors and . . . removed from his family within and nature without: a sanctuary, sacred and sterile."[5]

Lincoln uses Blossom as a convenient scapegoat for his fear of unmediated reality, but to do so he must remain blind to what she is, does, and says. For example, Blossom wants to delay dinner since she knows that Lincoln is at the crucial stage of beginning a new poem, but Lincoln acts as if she were insisting that the meal be served on time, and patronizingly remarks, "Literature must conform to dinner. Keep your values, Blossom" (12). He refuses to see that such conformity is not one of Blossom's values, but that of the patriarchy, the law of the fathers, which is embodied in his employer, Blossom's father. Lincoln maintains her in the style to which he believes she wishes to stay accustomed because "I'll not have your father say you married a damn poet, and have to live in a cellar, or a garret" (13). What is even more disconcerting is the way Blossom sometimes feels as if she were her father's representative and somehow responsible for his ruthless deeds, such as cutting down a beautiful wood to get clay for his cement works. In the face of Lincoln's criticism, voiced to her, not to her father, "Blossom was too hurt to speak, as if, being her father's fault, it must be her fault" (22).

Similarly, Lincoln wants his mother to play the role of an adoring and grateful old lady, saved from poverty by a dutiful son who has sacrificed time for his poetry in order to support her. In reality,

Mrs. Holt is a perfectly self-sufficient woman who supported and educated her son through a career in teaching, which she very much enjoyed. As her criticism of Lincoln's poetry indicates, she recognizes his evasiveness and refuses to conform to his script. As in the case of his relationship with Blossom, Mrs. Holt's behavior is not the real issue for Lincoln; he is worried about another father, his own, who deserted his wife and son twenty-seven years ago in order to free himself from the strictures of conformity. In doing so, Ambrose Holt gave his wife the chance to be the independent and accomplished woman she is, but Lincoln does not see it that way; he wants to best his father. "His father had been a writer, of a sort, and not gone very far with it. The son would be a real writer, and support the family" (32).

As Blossom painfully observes Lincoln's struggles with his father-in-law and father, she is confronted with the problem of how to rear her own sons so that they will not be similarly tortured. Lincoln's experienced mother would be an obvious source of counsel, but, as in the case of many of Glaspell's pioneers, her trials have hardened her, at least on the surface, so that she is a woman who "shuts herself in with so much composure, such authority" (97).

Blossom also wants to be a strong mother, as evidenced in her insistence that the boys call her "Mother" instead of "Mummie" (10). Her problem, or challenge, is exacerbated because her four-year-old, Paul, "had suffered a children's disease, and might never move as his brother did" (10). Lincoln wants young Lincoln, the six-year-old, to defer to Paul because "the strong must be chivalrous" (78). Blossom knows that "it's not good for his character" (78). She wants the boys to interact from genuine affection, not the laws of chivalry:

> Blossom did not like the idea of sacrifice, though she could not
> have said why, or rather, would not have permitted herself to
> know why. One should not know that it was sacrifice; one should
> know only that it was love, and natural to do (10).

She does not want to acknowledge the way young Lincoln's relationship with Paul resembles the way his father treats her, as signaled by Lincoln's choice of the word "chivalrous," which indicates his deference to her "handicap," her gender.

The uneasily maintained status quo is shattered by the impulsive return of Lincoln's father, who is living in a boardinghouse in an undesirable part of town. When Blossom decides to seek him out, she finds someone who will treat her as an adult, call her Harriette, and take her concerns seriously, or, in other words, be the father she needs at that point. He tells her he left because "they knew just who I was and they expected me to be just that, and that is a little as if they were putting a pillow on my face and sitting on it" (104). Blossom is inspired by his example to break out of the deadening script others have written for her, but, because she has what she calls "a sense of responsibility" (105), she tries to free others along with herself.

Blossom first attempts to demonstrate her maturity by rewriting her role in the marriage. Instead of serving as Lincoln's scapegoat for the inane conformity of society, she cancels several social engagements so that he will have more time to begin his new poem. Because she does not want to upset him at this delicate stage of his work, she does not tell him about the cancelled plans, nor, for the same reason, does she inform him that his father is back in town and that she has met and enjoyed talking with him. Her rebellion is only in its tentative beginnings, and she is still frightened by the prospect of Lincoln's defensively jealous wrath because, though it seems incredible to this reader, she loves him so much.

Blossom does have the courage to confront her father, but at this point, only for Lincoln's sake. Her father is a self-made man, a workaholic who constantly needs to prove that he is superior to his wife, a well-born Charlestonian who surrendered her autonomy and overeats because "there was little enough to do, anyway" (57). Her father is aggressive in his defense of his lifestyle because, as Blossom muses, "she agreed with her father, he should have been a really great inventor—not just cashed in so easily" (56). In her parents' marriage, Blossom may subconsciously perceive where her own union is heading: Lincoln would eventually abandon his poetry and take over his father-in-law's business, and she would become his bored, boring, and useless status symbol.

When Blossom goes to see her father to ask that he help her keep Lincoln unaware of his father's return until his poem is well under way, she is enacting a pattern of literary daughterhood described by Lynda Zwinger in *Daughters, Fathers, and the Novel.*

The father, in these and other versions of Western, middle-class family stories, always has a question he will neither articulate nor take responsibility for. The daughter strives to discover and then answer satisfactorily (or not) the form the paternal question seems to take in her particular relation to her father. Whether she answers yes or no, the daughter is positioned as the one who provokes the question, who *makes* the unspoken story happen.[6]

Blossom is asking, and answering, her father's unspoken question about the value of creativity, the creativity that he renounced, but that Lincoln still precariously retains. She stresses this, their true question, by opposing the destruction of the woods in which Lincoln finds poetic inspiration and by stating that Lincoln "shouldn't be in business at all!" (90). Her father implicitly defends his own mistaken choice by taking the "high" ground of patriarchy, calling her "a silly little girl" (86) and commenting that "Women *are* silly, and that makes a great deal of trouble" (91–92).

When Lincoln later learns of Blossom's pleasurable meeting with his father, he acts like a petulant version of Blossom's own father. He feels that she has betrayed him by taking his father's side against him, though neither Blossom nor his father see any "sides" at all. Like an Oedipus in reverse, he cries, "My father has taken my wife away from me!" (116). He uses his patriarchal status to remind Blossom of her place when he accuses her of being "a wife who won't stand by her husband" (118). As he vents his vituperation by calling Blossom "a stupid, meddling, conceited, little —" (119), he is interrupted by the entrance of his mother, who defends Blossom and says that she herself has seen and will continue to see her newly returned husband. Lincoln threatens to throw his mother out if she persists in her course, but, like Gordon Wallace at the end of *Woman's Honor*, he is the one to surrender in the face of united women; he leaves the room and the women have dinner together.

As is typical of a Glaspell heroine's progress toward autonomy, Blossom's timidity returns and she suffers a setback. As is also typical of Glaspell's work, Blossom's regression is provoked by her fears for her sons since in the world as she knows it, they are her only hope, her only possible contribution.[7] As she watches them sleeping, she muses,

No matter what might break up in confusion, this important thing, at the center, remained, and must be guarded. So nothing very terrible could happen. . . . You had to keep in your place, even though, in that place, you weren't felt for what you felt yourself to be. A woman should not be conceited, and vaguely wistful, and the Ambrose Holts were fools, and malignant. So she could feel in the room where her two sons slept, sleeping through the disturbance and unhappiness around them (139–40).

The use of the word "center" here is significant, for after further talks with her mother-in-law and Ambrose Holt, Blossom decides, "She had gotten loose; she was *out*; she couldn't go back, for it would not be the same self she took back" (203). She has become one of Glaspell's women on the edge, "the outside," or "the verge," and she stimulates the knee-jerk reflex of traditional men to such women when her enraged father tells her she is *"crazy"* (194) and threatens to disinherit her and her sons.

Blossom is forced to develop her own resources and become self-reliant since her masculine props have deserted her: her biological father is furious, her father-husband Lincoln has left for New York to sulk in the company of the pretentiously intellectual Margot Epstein, and her spiritual father, Ambrose Holt, has disappeared again. Even more important is Blossom's realization that her idol, Lincoln, has feet of clay. A visiting critic, Hugh Parker, tells her that Lincoln has led him to assume that Blossom was an invalid since she did not accompany him on his trips to New York, journeys which Blossom has always longed to make. Parker also expected to find the world of Babbitt, but he is pleasantly surprised by Blossom and her circle of friends. One of Lincoln's male golf companions tells Parker and Blossom that "sometimes, over a drink, I'd like to talk about a book. Then [Lincoln] gives me the razzberry. I may not be much, but why make me less than I am?" (237). Parker realizes that Lincoln has used a similar strategy on his New York friends: "He feels he really has it on us, because he is what we aren't. It's superior, really, except that it's wistful" (239).

When Blossom perceives the damage to her husband from her father's patriarchal demands and his own father's whimsical neglect, she decides to rebel against Lincoln's method of childrearing. She also realizes what her privileged life has made her and ironically acknowledges that her father was right: "As he said, she had been shielded, she knew nothing about life. And now she was going to pass that on to her sons" (210). She notices that she is raising future patriarchs who will tyrannize women and the less privileged; already "they were arrogant, impertinent to the servants" (210). When young Lincoln tells her that he will never have to work because his grandfather has so much money, Blossom tells him that "he may leave it to orphan boys. . . . who have good manners" (211); in other words, his status as male heir will be meaningless in the world of kindness and consideration that she wants the future to be.

As Blossom recognizes that men, young and old, are not inscrutable gods, she begins to realize the strength that can be found in women. In Lincoln's absence, she becomes much closer to her mother-in-law, particularly as they share Hugh Parker's two thank-you gifts, a biography of Emily Dickinson and Virginia Woolf's *A Room of One's Own*. In their lives and works, both Dickinson and Woolf exemplify what women can accomplish when they have their own space, a nurturing environment like a womb in which they are both mother and child, not a tomb-like refuge from life such as Lincoln's room. As Glaspell demonstrated in *Alison's House*, writers like Dickinson and Woolf "said it — for women," especially those women, including Blossom and Mrs. Holt, who have artists' powers of feeling without their powers of expression.[8]

The death of Ambrose Holt provides the final impetus to Blossom's growth. He has willed his end by refusing to inject the insulin he needs to treat his diabetes. In a long letter to Blossom, he explains his life's successes and failures and exhorts her to "see the world around you, Harriette. Love life, and don't let any of them fool you" (281). As his use of her true name indicates, he sees her as the woman she is capable of becoming: mature, strong, and compassionate. As Arthur E. Waterman points out, "In the gift of his death, Ambrose, like Bernice, offers the best expression of his life."[9] In some ways, Ambrose's gift is even better than that of the title character of Glaspell's 1919 play because no deception is involved and Blossom is a much more worthy recipient than Bernice's selfish husband. In any case, Ambrose acts as a father who helps a daughter to mature, unlike Blossom's own father who wants her to remain a child.

At the end of the novel, Blossom seems in control. She directs that Ambrose be buried from her and Lincoln's home, and both Lincoln and her father acquiesce. Lincoln calls Blossom "so good" (306) and Margot Epstein a "fool" (302). Her methods of childrearing are also now accepted by Lincoln, who even suggests that they now might try to have a daughter. Blossom, however, knows that "it will not always be like this," that "it would slip back" (314), but, as the last lines of the book suggest, the struggle would be shared by equals: "Lincoln had waited for her and they went on together" (315).

Despite the happy ending, *Ambrose Holt and Family* raises more questions than it resolves. Throughout the novel, even on the penultimate page, the narrator refers to the protagonist as Blossom. Perhaps this nomenclature indicates that not until the last page has Blossom earned the right to name herself Harriette, but it also suggests that Glaspell is wearily resigned to the subservient status of women, as is also indicated in the peculiar spelling of *Harriette*: the final *t* and *e* seem to reinforce the name's inferior status as a diminutive and a feminine version of the male name Harry. The name *Blossom*, though puerile, at least suggests the heroine's womanhood and her potential to bear fruit. The conflicting messages sent by the heroine's names may show that at the beginning of the 1930s, Glaspell sees no names, identities, or roles for women that do not diminish them in invidious comparisons with men.

Another masculine name also erases that of the heroine since the novel is called *Ambrose Holt and Family*. Although Ambrose Holt is the catalyst for much of the action, there is no doubt that the novel's protagonist is Harriette "Blossom" Holt, who has the courage to act on Ambrose's ideas and the greater courage to do so without deserting those who could benefit from her actions and example. As in Glaspell's works of the late 1920s, we are left only with the hope that the sons Blossom raises will make a better world for men and women, a hope that unfortunately also serves to erase Blossom as a worthwhile individual in her own right. The modern reader may be repelled by Glaspell's vision, but we would be guilty of "presentism" if we reproached her since she was describing what she saw at the end of the 1920s, a decade of regression for women.

The 1930s was an even worse decade for Glaspell, as indicated by the eight-year gap between her novels. Her pain over her childlessness was exacerbated by her loss of Norman Matson to a pregnant teenager. She suffered from alcoholism, writer's block, and financial difficulties. In addition, as Arthur E. Waterman points out, Glaspell's type of fiction is "distinctly separate from the novels of social protest and political ideology, works of a highly topical intention, which were being written during this decade."[10] In an attempt to break through her writer's block, she returned to the Midwest to direct that region's Federal Theater Project, but the reading of hundreds of plays did not leave her much time for her own work, and she returned to Provincetown in May of 1938.[11] Her second and last novel of the 1930s, *The Morning Is Near Us* (1939) concerns a woman who learns to live a meaningful life without a man, Glaspell's own difficult lesson during that decade.

Like *Ambrose Holt and Family*, *The Morning Is Near Us* concerns a woman's need to come to terms with her fathers, biological and nonbiological. Like *Brook Evans*, it also stresses a maternal legacy, but, unlike the rebellious and intensely maternal Naomi Kellogg of *Brook Evans*, the mother in this novel, Hertha Chippman, displays indifference toward her daughter and capitulates to her husband's desire to exile the girl. Like *Fugitive's Return*, *The Morning Is Near Us* begins *in medias res*, but the heroine, Lydia Chippman, is not about to kill herself, but plans to start a new life as she returns to her home after two decades of wandering around the world. At first, the novel seems to be a sunny depiction of the way a latter-day cosmopolitan Pollyanna overcomes small-town small-mindedness, but the mood darkens when Lydia, who believes her father is dead, cannot find his grave. Glaspell then uses flashbacks to establish the past, but a consideration of the novel's events in chronological order demonstrates the intergenerational patterns.

In the founding father of the Chippman clan, Glaspell once again depicts a pioneer like *Inheritors*' Silas Morton, but this time negatively. Ezra Chippman chose a secluded site for his homestead "because a man could be by himself here, and since then the Chippmans had been a good deal by themselves."[12] This is not Thoreauvian contemplation of spirit in the midst of nature, but misanthropy, a fleeing from others because one is fearful and awkward when dealing with them. The effect on the family's women is reminiscent of the state of the isolated farm women in *Trifles*. In the next generation, Betsy Chippman had planted a double row of cedars because "a person had to do something, she'd said" (4). She also kept up her spirits by taking in a runaway orphan, Hertha, whom she raised with her own son John. This generous action leads to tragedy as if she had invoked a curse by violating the paternal taboo against outsiders.

Hertha herself has been violated, both by fate and a man. After her loving parents were drowned, she was separated from her intensely beloved brother Joe when he was adopted and she was sent to the cold Larson family as a hired girl. The eerily beautiful young girl repeatedly attempted to run away in order to find her brother, though she knew neither his whereabouts nor his adopted name. In one of her many unsent letters to her brother, she later relates that on one of these escapes, "There was one man was *bad* to me. He said I was to be his little girl, but he was a bad man" (157–58).

Although Hertha stated that the man was bad, she also believed that she herself is somehow bad as a result of the molestation, a too-common reaction of victims of rape and sexual abuse. This guilt caused her to act in ways that add to her guilt and misery in an endless vicious circle. When adopted by the Chippmans at age eleven, she maintained a defensive silence. A schoolmate later recalls, "There was something about her kept you from asking questions. Those who did ask — got silence for their pains" (124). When she was fifteen, she refused the attentions of the local boys, even Fred Ayres to whom she was strongly attracted. In her last letter to her brother, she writes, "I think I'd like boys and like them to like me, but I don't think I should, do you? Because it makes me different — what happened — doesn't it?" (167–68).

Hertha regarded the secluded Chippman home as her refuge, the place where she could hide what she considered her guilty secret, but her defensiveness once again led to increased guilt. Her fortress was breached from within when John Chippman took advantage of her naiveté, fear, and guilt to trick her into marrying him after his parents' death. The only way they could stay in the house together, he claimed, was by marrying since she was not his blood kin. Because Hertha regarded John as her brother, she regarded herself as even more guilty for violating the incest taboo (281). After she had one child by John, a son named Wayne, Hertha tried to cleanse herself by affairs with other men, one of which results in Lydia.

The Chippman house itself becomes a symbol of that family's legacy of reclusiveness and of Hertha's guilt. Ezra's decision to build in a spot hidden by hills meant that the house could get little sun, and succeeding generations kept making additions, which they hoped would get more light. The result is a house that looked "like an ill-formed bird" (7) because "the two later builders had not worked in harmony with the man who built first" (6); it represents the way the reclusive Chippmans can neither soar out for contact with others nor maintain harmony among themselves by meaningful communication. John adds a wing so that Hertha can get the evening sun, but this change is the only one the couple makes. Decades later their son Wayne observes that "nothing got thrown out. Mother and Father seemed to want it to stay just as it was" (9). Both Hertha and John want to keep the house as it was before their marriage when they were happy together as brother and sister.

Stasis is death, for the marriage and for the Chippman place, as another aspect of the farm indicates. On one side of the house, the Chippmans kept selling land to the town for the cemetery. John continued that tradition, since, as Wayne remembers, "Father had lost heart and didn't care about land as most farmers did. The dead needed it, was all he'd said" (5). After Hertha's death, John killed a hired man who attempted to blackmail him with Hertha's reputation and was incarcerated in a mental asylum. He deeded the Chippman place to the now thirty-two-year-old Lydia if she returned to claim it in three years; if she failed to do so, it would go to the town for the cemetery. This gesture could be regarded as an attempt to compensate Lydia for her loveless childhood, but it also associates her with the cemetery as if she were the final repository of John's dead hopes for Hertha's love.

As John knows nothing of Hertha's childhood molestation, so Lydia as a child knows nothing of the reasons for her parents' unhappiness. Unfortunately, like Hertha after the sexual abuse, Lydia somehow feels she is to blame, and so a new generation begins its cycle of ignorance and guilt. Hertha's treatment of her daughter is largely responsible for Lydia's low self-esteem. Wayne remembers the way "his mother had turned abruptly from Lydia, who was asking for something" (32). John's Aunt Jenifer witnesses such behavior and takes Lydia to live with her. At her departure, Hertha "kissed Lydia, but then she drew away; she didn't hold her, as you'd think a mother would when her young daughter—not sixteen—was going away" (33).

This lack of maternal validation makes Lydia feel so insubstantial, so worthless, that she can commit herself neither to a place nor a person for the next twenty years. She travels somewhat aimlessly in Europe, Asia, Africa, and Mexico, but "she couldn't get away from a no doubt needless idea that she wasn't to have a home. . . . It is hard to feel at home in a new life when you are left bewildered about the old one" (51). She has a serious affair with a married man, Henri, but he turns away from her with these words:

> Something is wrong with you. You are too pure. You are cold—though I don't think you are really cold. But guarded—withdrawn. And you look as if underneath the reserve there waited—waited to flame and leap—. . . . You don't even know what I'm talking about, do you? You might live with one hundred men and you would never give yourself! (49–50).

Despite his sexist demand that she give herself, Henri is accurately observing the results of Hertha's treatment of Lydia. The mother who turns away when her daughter asks for something is acting as if Lydia is not there; as a result, Lydia believes she has no self to give. What Henri calls "cold" and "pure" is Lydia's psyche frozen in a state of immaturity because she has "guarded" herself from the emotional commitments that she fears will expose her vacuity as mercilessly as Henri does.

As Lydia approaches her mid-thirties, she receives three gifts that seem to betoken happier days. From an elderly man, Joseph Blake, who had known her mother in the days when he worked on the railroad near the Chippman home, she inherits ten thousand dollars. She does not know that the man might be her mother's long-lost brother Joe or even her father if he had been one of Hertha's lovers, and she does not attempt to learn his motivation. Because of some condolences from a hometown acquaintance whom she met in Rome, Lydia mistakenly assumes that John Chippman, the man she believes to be her father, is dead so that she also assumes that the conditional bequest of the Chippman homestead is part of his will and an act of love toward her. She decides to give herself the gift of children and adopts Koula from

Greece and Diego from Mexico because "she wouldn't have her own children, for she wasn't going to defraud another man as Henri felt she had defrauded him" (52). In spite of her acknowledgement to the children that "the Indians were not fairly treated" (107) by the Anglo settlers, she still tells them that America is a "great country, where we can be . . . happy and free" (108).

Since Lydia's happiness is based on a willed ignorance of unhappy facts, it is predictably blasted as she begins the search for knowledge of her antecedents, a quest that was sparked by her inability to locate John Chippman's grave where she expects to find it, next to her mother in the cemetery on the side of the homestead. In a predictable plot, Lydia would grow as she learns every important fact about John and Hertha, but Glaspell makes Lydia a much more complex and credible character because she portrays her as too naive, too paralyzed in her immaturity, to plumb the depths of her initial discoveries. She finds her mother's unsent letters to her brother Joe but does not seem to realize that her mother is discussing sexual abuse; Lydia seems to assume that when her mother writes about her experiences making her different, she is referring to her tragic life in general. About her mother's withdrawal from others, Lydia naively draws this conclusion: "It wasn't necessary. That boy—Fred Ayres—wouldn't have cared. He would have been fascinated by the story, and so would [Hertha's] girl friend, Mary" (175). Similarly, she believes that John's pathological obsession with Hertha was avoidable: "Surely you can love as much and still love others near you. More. It should make you love them more" (191).

At thirty-five, Lydia is too old to play Pollyanna, but only unmediated madness and hatred can finally shock her out of her willful romantic ignorance. When she learns that John Chippman, whom she still believes to be her father, is in the mental asylum, she decides to visit him, but the sight of what appears to be his catatonic state so paralyzes her that she can neither approach him nor leave.

> Now she knew separateness. It was a loneliness such as she had never known could be. There he sat, and she did not know how to reach him, and she was frozen too and could not try. Never before had she really understood—We live alone. It plumbed the depth of the loneliness of the human soul (216).

Not quite the depth, however, since when Lydia writes to John Chippman, his reply is full of bitter hatred against her. He tells her the truth about her origins and that she should "go away now" (246).

In accordance with the Glaspell heroine's typical pattern of growth, Lydia at first regresses after the letter from John Chippman. As if signaling the imminent death of her soul, she decides to let the cemetery have the homestead and move herself, Koula, and Diego far away in spite of the happiness the children have expressed in their new home. Of her mother she asks herself, "How could you cherish memory of a woman who would turn from her own child at command of any man?" (254). She is venting her anger on the wrong object: she cannot perceive her mother as a victim of life and men because she is still so obsessed with what she perceives as her own victimization by Hertha.

Marcia Noe comments that in *The Morning Is Near Us*, Glaspell "sets the stage for tragedy but only hints at the climax and stops short of the denouement."[13] In an apparently happy ending, John Chippman escapes from the asylum and tells Lydia that he and Hertha had really loved her, but out of their love and consideration for each other, "she thought she couldn't show she loved you — though she *did* — she did, Lydia; and I couldn't show it. . . ." (289). He then dies with Hertha's name on his lips, and, in the last line of the novel, Lydia is "glad of that" (296); she is Pollyanna once more.

Like the conclusion of *Ambrose Holt and Family*, this novel's ending is not a truly happy one since the heroine also rebels only briefly and appears content to have her own hopes erased, in this case in favor of the generations that precede and follow her. Lydia seems willing to surrender her right to a happy childhood and normal maturity to the love that John and Hertha maintained at her expense. She will live for the next generation, in the form of a symbolic son, Diego, for Koula, her adopted daughter, is a conformist who "wanted to be like the people around her"; in contrast, Diego asks questions and wants to keep his name and his past as part of becoming an American (45, 46).

Also as in the case of *Ambrose Holt and Family*, the novel's title erases its heroine as it subsumes her in a vague *Us*. This group could be the humanity who is waiting for strong yet sensitive males, like Diego, to bring about the dawn of a new order. If the pronoun, however, refers to the women, that morning had been near them in the suffrage struggles of the Progressive Era and would dawn again during the feminist movement of the 1960s, but for the women of Lydia's generation, it was always tantalizingly in sight but never within reach.

8

Older, Wiser, and Sadder: Glaspell's Female *Reifungsromane*

In the 1940s, Susan Glaspell presented her final perspective on a century of American women in a children's book, *Cherished and Shared of Old* (1940), and two novels, *Norma Ashe* (1942) and *Judd Rankin's Daughter* (1946).[1] As she approached and entered her eighth decade, the world seemed to be repeating history as if oblivious to its lessons. Another world war recalled questions about the relative values of engagement and isolationism. For women, these problems were again intensified and complicated since they were expected to experience the war through their men. Should they beg their men to find safe jobs or admonish them to return with their shields or on them?

Glaspell uses this recurrent nightmare of war to explore the nature of aging in women. In *From the Hearth to the Open Road: A Feminist Study of Aging in Contemporary Literature*, Barbara Frey Waxman calls such a work a *Reifungsroman* or the "novel of ripening."[2] Although Waxman is discussing fiction written after the resurgence of feminism in the 1960s, many of the characteristics that she identifies can be found in Glaspell's works of the 1940s, particularly the motif of the journey.

> Whether or not they are literally travelling, these protagonists usually make an internal journey to their past through dreams and frequent flashbacks, essential features of the *Reifungsroman*

narrative structure. As they travel, they gradually come to terms with crucial decisions they made as youths; with past experiences, often sexual, that influenced their lives; and with their cultural roots. Then they try to chart a new course either into or through old age, which they embark on at the end of the work.[3]

Glaspell's fiction of the forties varies from this pattern, however, in that it focuses on the future of others, as well as that of the protagonist, through her use of the maternal metaphor.

Glaspell's first work of the 1940s, *Cherished and Shared of Old*, is a children's book written to promote the assistance of European refugees. Its title and epigraph are taken from George Cram Cook's translation of some lines from Sappho:

> Though we know that never a longing mortal
> Gains life['s] best — Oh, better it is to pray for
> Part in what we cherished and shared of old than
> Fail to remember.[4]

This passage suggests that memory promotes the cherishing of the good, but much of the story concerns the tenacious hold of old hatred, greed, and prejudice on the present through the stories of two middle-aged midwestern farm women and neighbors, Addie Morrison and Emma Schultz.

In their youth, Addie and Emma were the best of friends but were later divided by their fathers who quarreled over a piece of land between the farms. The Schultz family won the legal battle and prospered; the losing Morrisons' fortunes continued to decline. The women lost even more when Emma's fiance, Addie's brother Walter, was killed in the First World War. For decades Addie and Emma perpetuated the domestic and foreign battles of their menfolk despite their love for and need of each other. As the story opens at the beginning of World War II, Addie Morrison, now a widow, tries to keep her hatred of Emma and her family alive by recalling an old prejudice that is revived by the current war. When Emma's dog appears at the Morrison farm, Addie tries to send him back, crying "Bad German dog."[5] As they prepare for Christmas, Addie reluctantly acknowledges that "no one had ever taken Emma's place" while on the Schultz place Emma thinks, "Ten thousand times she'd wished that land in the bottom of the sea."

As is so characteristic of Glaspell's fiction, the women are reunited by their hopes for the future as embodied in children. Addie has given refuge to two Dutch war orphans, Johanna and Piet, at the behest of her grown daughter, Emma Schultz's namesake, who is working for such displaced children in the East. When Addie sees the orphans' delight in the Schultz dog, she softens and allows them to play with it, and even to put a red ribbon around its neck. When the dog returns home, Emma interprets the ribbon as goodwill sign from Addie. As she remembers her own trials as an immigrant girl and the way Addie had befriended her, Emma decides to bring cookies to the Dutch children, and the women's friendship is rekindled. As the last line of the story suggests, Glaspell seems to hope that what happened for these individuals can happen to a world on the brink of war: "Fear flew out through the window when love came in by the door."

Cherished and Shared of Old is a slight piece with its implausibly sudden happy ending, but it indicates the alternate routes that are available to the heroines of Glaspell's last two novels. Like Emma and Addie before their reconciliation, Norma Ashe clings to the beliefs of the past without finding any practical means of bringing its positive values into the future. In contrast, like the reunited Addie and Emma, Frances Rankin Mitchell, *Judd Rankin's Daughter*, uses her practical and emotional skills as a mother to revivify what was "cherished and shared of old" for succeeding generations.

The woman Glaspell presents at the beginning of *Norma Ashe* appears a parody of motherhood, unable to cherish or share anything at all. Mrs. Utterbach is the shrill and shabby proprietor of a boardinghouse in a once genteel, now run-down neighborhood in Iroquois City, Illinois. Her idea of maternal concern is attempting to prevent her daughter Lorna from associating with her boarders, whom she calls "riffraff," because she wants Lorna to be a part of the town's high society though they can no longer afford it.[6] When a crippled young woman who is behind in her rent begs to keep her room, Mrs. Utterbach refuses to perform one of those nonbiologically maternal acts that Glaspell so prizes; she responds, "I have my own children to think about" (13).

As Mrs. Utterbach screams at the coal man because he will not deliver the coal without cash in advance, she fails to notice another seeker of nurture, a well-dressed visitor in her parlor. Her closest college friend has sought Norma Ashe Utterbach in the hope that Norma will reinspire her youthful idealism, but she cannot see Norma in the enviously materialistic Mrs. Utterbach. Nor can Norma herself, who, jolted from her rut by Rosie's visit, begins her search for her lost self. "She was trying to find out what ever became of Norma Ashe. She really did not know, and for some reason she could not have given, she had to know" (66).

In an extended flashback, Glaspell traces Norma's path in becoming a woman whom her earlier self would have abhorred. At the significantly named Pioneer College, she and Rosie had belonged to a small group of disciples who clustered around a charismatic philosophy teacher, Joseph Langley. His brand of idealism is difficult to identify from the novel, as if by this point Glaspell was too disappointed by too many "isms" to delineate the specifics of one more, but it involves George Cram Cook's belief that like the creatures that made a great leap from water to land, so human beings were about to make an evolutionary leap in spiritual progress (104, 318–19). Under Langley's tutelage, Norma apparently experiences some sort of mystical vision of this future (71). Although Langley died before his disciples graduated from college, he believed he had prepared them to promote and benefit from the evolutionary leap, which Norma compares to an "unborn child" (104). Norma is to attend graduate school at the University of Chicago on scholarship and become a college teacher, a spiritual mother who would nurture the ideals of others.

Norma loses her ideals and identity, not through selfishness or evil, but through chance, love, and maternal feeling, all of which Glaspell believes are genuine parts of life that can be denied only by denying life itself. As she leaves Pioneer College, Norma meets Max Utterbach when their train is delayed and rerouted by a wreck on the line. This chance encounter leads to love:

> The passion that grew between them . . . all sweeping into the passion of man for woman, woman for man, the hot sharp need to weld into one that frightened them both, making them so nearly one it was almost the same, almost as if already they had merged their lives and there could be no drawing back before what was and had to be (119).

As this description indicates, Glaspell is not denying that passion is a necessary part of life, but is suggesting the threat to individual identity if this merging is mistaken for all of life, a threat to which women are culturally conditioned to be more vulnerable.

Maternal feeling, that essential component of Glaspell's vision of the life-force, can be a similar trap. Max is on the same train with Norma because he is taking his mother's coffin for burial. He is not only grief-stricken but guilt-stricken since his obsessive quest for wealth prevented him from giving her the attention that he owed her. He attempts to replace his mother with Norma when he wants her to be happy for his success "because . . . my mother can't be" (116). Norma seems oblivious to the warning inherent in Max's neglect of his mother and accepts the role. She considers him her "first pupil" (103) whose eyes "clung to her — incredulous, hurt, imploring" (91), like those of a child.

Glaspell presents Norma with mutually exclusive choices: either Norma becomes a scholar and surrenders her capacities as a wife and mother or she sacrifices her career and her very identity for these familial roles. Norma fights the constriction of her potential but eventually makes the latter choice. As a newlywed in Texas, it "still seemed strange when she and Max were referred to as the Utterbachs" (136), but because of his need for her and her love for him, she eventually becomes resigned to the fact that "I can't be myself and be his wife" (165). She even seems to accept Max's relegation of her ideals to the realm of domestic trivia when he tells her, "You keep the dream and let me make the money" (166). His shady dealings in Texas cause them to move suddenly to Illinois where his reckless pursuit of money leads to risky investments. Max is killed as he impatiently tries to fix a piece of equipment in his plant as if money could not be produced fast enough. Norma, a bankrupt widow with two small children, begins her decline into the hag-like keeper of the boardinghouse.

Norma is now reduced to one domestic role, that of mother, but her increasingly narrow interpretation of that part causes her to fail her children.[7] Her first son, Langley's namesake Joseph, is stillborn like the dreams she inherited from his ghostly father. Her second son Fred is named after her husband's partner in a crooked business deal and follows that path into bootlegging. Her daughter Lorna is good-hearted but frivolous: "'I like to have fun,' she'd say, and as if it weren't very important to her where she had it" (25). Norma has so subsumed her identity in that of Max that she never taught her children the idealism she cherished in her youth. They learned well what she did teach them: Max's obsession with social status and wealth emerge in Fred as materialism and in Lorna as hedonism.

Glaspell shows an alternate route for Norma in one of her fellow disciples, Helen Foster, who chose a career as a settlement house worker. In response to Norma's query about how she has enacted Langley's ideals, Helen writes:

> I work very hard—often washing children's clothes, giving them baths, trying to teach them not to steal; anything that's to be done. . . . Perhaps all we can do is the little thing that's at hand, even though it's only taking lice out of a poor child's head (174).

In response, Norma muses, "So much gets left out. . . . We start to do our little thing, and in that we lead our busy lives" (174). If we accept Norma's interpretation of Helen as one who has lost her idealistic vision in the quasi-domestic "little things" of social work, the two women's situations resemble that of the two heroines of *Bernice*: Margaret Pierce is a busy social activist who needs to be reminded of the purpose of her activity by the saintly but passive Bernice. Time, the two decades that separate *Bernice* and *Norma Ashe*, and another world war may have compelled Glaspell to question Bernice's form of passive, suicidal idealism. Norma's failure to put her ideals to use in the world does not make her into the divine Bernice but the shrewish Mrs. Utterbach. Helen Foster seems much happier, more fulfilled, in her socially useful nonbiological maternity.

As Waxman observes, the heroines of *Reifungsromane* must undertake a journey in order to progress spiritually. At the nadir of her character, shortly after Rosie's visit, Norma travels from Iroquois City to Chicago to sell the diamond Max had given her, her last keepsake from him, to free her son Fred from jail on a bootlegging charge. This maternal act spurs her to relinquish Max and his values with the jewel: she vows never to return to Iroquois City and takes a job as the hired "girl" at a Chicago boardinghouse. Although she has fallen even farther in social status, she begins her spiritual ascent. When she hears one of Langley's disciples, Austin Wurthen, lecture at the University of Chicago, she recognizes that this factory owner has twisted Langley's words to use them in support of paternalistic capitalism, a honeyed-over exploitation of the workers. She rises in the lecture hall and denounces this perversion of Langley's teachings and so regains her true jewel, her idealistic vision, which she had traded for Max's diamond. "Not as that which has faded did she see it now, but like a diamond, imperishable, forever lighted from within itself" (236).

At this point, Norma is ready to nurture the child of her spirit who, as is typical of Glaspell's late work, is a male since women's experience as Glaspell depicts it makes them unable to live the dream; they can only convey it to culturally privileged young men. After her ejection from Wurthen's lecture, Norma is approached by a student, Scott Neubolt, who is genuinely curious about the wisdom hidden beneath the exterior of an impoverished washerwoman. He finds her a better job at his sister's house and "the new friend — youth of today — welcomed Norma back to the world" (280). Although Norma once more loses her faith when she receives the false information that Langley mocked his disciples behind their backs, she leaves Chicago and returns to Iroquois City rather than disillusion Scott. Her refusal to tell Scott the truth suggests that she senses that even if Langley were false to them, his ideals could still be valid; at this point, Norma is simply too old, warped, and bitter to sort it out for herself and explain it to Scott.

As if to reinforce her message about women's socially enforced inability to realize ideals, Glaspell has Norma return to the boardinghouse at Iroquois City shortly before the birth of her granddaughter, Lorna's child Mary, named for the mother of the charlatan chiropractor Lorna has married. As she bathes the baby, Norma mentally exhorts her:

> Have courage. Baby, do not let them kill the best that is in you. Be pure. Be strong. Be dauntless, Mary. Love the things around you: the flowers, the stars, your fellow-man. So will joy come, and faith. And the other may come too. Oh, I hope so! Your look . . . into the meaning (345).

Norma's hopes seem unfounded since she is not speaking aloud, the infant would be too young to understand her anyway, and Norma hands the child back to her mother, the vulgar Lorna, and so back into the realm of her materially focused father. Mary will never receive her ideals since Norma dies shortly after this scene.

Glaspell's endings are often problematic, but the conclusion of Norma Ashe seems particularly ambiguous. When Lorna's husband finds a box of Norma's college books and notebooks and brings them to her out of his rough kindness, she believes that he is mocking her. Her anger at him has the cathartic effect of snapping her out of her lethargy. She vows, "This time I will see *all the way.* . . . And it was not herself, after an hour, raised her head from the place where it had come to rest" (349). On the one hand, since she dies attempting to reclaim her vision, Norma may have reclaimed her identity. On the other hand, her idealism has not helped her or her descendants to lead happier, more productive lives. Her idealism has changed neither the world nor her own circumstances. Only through Scott Neubolt, the new bolt of lightning, does the hope of future change remain alive. In *Norma Ashe*, another one of Glaspell's "happy" endings, perhaps contrived for a popular audience, proves quite the opposite when examined in the context of the novel as a whole.

In contrast to the post-1960s feminist *Reifungsromane* analyzed by Waxman, Glaspell in *Norma Ashe* presents old age as too late for any meaningful changes. As if in recoil from this dismal vision, in her final novel, *Judd Rankin's Daughter*, Glaspell returns to a stage of life when hopes may still be realized, middle-age. As Waxman notes, a woman may find in mid-life "new independence, increasing ability to express herself, and courage to try new roles."[8] Glaspell's description of her heroine evokes the happy medium of this stage:

> Competent and kind. . . . People banked on her, and so it was fortunate she was strong. You looked into her eyes and knew she would not let you down: intelligent and honest eyes—kind, amused; an open, candid face, but a native shrewdness—you had better not go too far. . . . Her movements were competent though somewhat abrupt—no languid grace here.[9]

Now that she is no longer valued solely for her appearance and sexuality, forty-four-year-old Frances Rankin Mitchell can come into her own through a series of trials that at once test and temper her strength and confidence, particularly as a mother.

Glaspell once again presents a century of American women as

she flanks Frances with the generations before and after her. Frances' mother Mary, her almost-mother Jennie, and her Cousin Adah represent women raised in the latter half of the nineteenth century. They were too late to be pioneers but too early to reap the relative freedoms of their twentieth-century heirs. Mary initially seems to embody the Victorian notion of the pure woman with no passionate interest in sex. As her husband Judd Rankin later muses, "She had a sweet reasonableness and believed sex was a part of life. . . . But when you have to reason sex into its place in life—this is not the path to rapture" (81). Mary's legacy to her daughter, though, indicates that there may have been more vitality and restlessness under her conventional surface than her husband realizes. When Frances is a child, Mary gives her a globe, as if telling her to explore the world: do as I say, not as I do.

The fate of Jennie, Judd Rankin's youthful flame, shows why Mary needs to take refuge in "sweet reasonableness." When Judd's uncle sees him kiss their hired girl, eighteen-year-old Jennie, he yells, "Whoring!" and "Bitch—" (79). Judd later recalls with chagrin, "And that was love as he had first known it" (79), but the consequences for Jennie were far more grave. Given her culture's alternatives of madonna or whore, Jennie took the seemingly safe role and "became one of those women like [Judd's] Aunt Maude, too good for life, no good to life" (79). Judd also remembers that "years later there was a scandal about a girl in her own home, and [Jennie] had her sent to the reform school, with pious relish" (79).

Judd's cousin, Adah Elwood Logan, though Jennie and Mary's contemporary, was somehow more attuned to the winds of change for women as the century ended. Her rebellions, however, were relatively mild and quite personal ones, which did not really help herself or other women. As a young woman, she turned down a wealthy suitor and took up with an alcoholic, fired college professor. After that relationship ended, she married beneath her class, but her husband Joe Logan became quite wealthy through his own talents and drive. As if still vaguely dissatisfied, for years she carried on an affair with an editorial writer, Miles Maxwell, under the pretext of going to Chicago to see her dentist. Adah's subterfuge does not indicate that she is a cynic; on the contrary, it shows her idealism, though it is the idealism of the sheltered and powerless.

Adah tells Judd, "we should be happy and make everyone else we can happy—because that makes us nicer people and if we were nicer people wouldn't that make the world better, Juddie?" (49).

In many ways, Adah's characterization resembles that of *Bernice*'s title character in that her personality, one of magnetic charm, is rendered through the memories of others since she is unconscious and dying when the novel begins. The male perspective on Adah, that of Judd Rankin, idealizes her in the same way the other characters in that play worship Bernice. Judd recalls of Adah: "She knew things without having to struggle for them, felt without having to pay for it—or not too much. The woman never reasoned! . . . I think maybe she was divine" (74). Obviously, Judd sees what he wants to see, an irrational female stereotype dispensing happiness to others; he fails to perceive how little her society offered her.

Glaspell indicates her final, reluctant rejection of passive idealists like Bernice, Norma Ashe, and Adah through the perspective of Frances, a modern woman. Although she would not go so far as her daughter Madeleine and consider Adah "hypocritical" and "a parasite" (24), Frances dislikes Adah's clandestine affair as showing that "Adah knew how to 'play the game'" (8). She disapproves of Adah's lifestyle of conspicuous consumption: "It had been all wrong—that time: a few people living in absurd feudal grandeur and thousands upon thousands working hard and not making the grade" (14). Frances also realizes that "even though [Adah had] had something like a salon . . . she would certainly not be rated an intellectual among people Frances knew now" (10). Despite these reservations about Adah, neither Glaspell nor Frances is guilty of "presentism" since they sympathetically present Adah as a woman of her day who needed to use charm and wiles to achieve any of her own ends. Frances concludes that Adah's life was "a happy light in a drab world" (9).

If the seemingly successful woman of Adah's day was forced to resort to seductive subterfuges, the rising generation, represented by Frances's daughter, Madeleine, seems gracelessly blunt. As her nickname "Maddie" suggests, she is not afraid to show her anger at "parasites," and "she liked to take hold of things and shake them hard—as that puppy that rag" (22). Maddie, though, is also trapped, at least temporarily, by the mores of her day since she feels it almost obligatory to rebel against convention with her melancholy and married suitor, Horace Saxon.

Although Glaspell's portraits of the women of Adah and Maddie's generations are meant to enhance the happy medium of the middle-aged Frances, Glaspell does not present all women of Frances's age as ideal. Frances has always admired her friend Marianna for being "stabilizing, giving a sense of things that would go on" (133). Her conservatism is revealed as reactionary when she refuses to sell her house to another of Frances's friends because Julia is Jewish. Julia, like *Bernice*'s Margaret Pierce, is a social activist, a worker for child refugees from war-torn Europe, who is so overworked and enmeshed by her cause that she sometimes forgets what it all means, the gift to the future of nonbiological maternity: "Each one of the children for whom Julia worked to give more air, more sunshine, more food and love, might have been Julia's child" (170). Julia needs a refuge, as she tells Frances, "to keep me . . . womanly" (171).

In this novel, Frances is presented as the golden mean for women. Unlike Marianna in her moated grange, she is conservative in the best sense of the word, one who preserves what was "cherished and shared of old." She states, "When I make jelly, or pickles . . . I am once more with all the women behind me" (97), who showed their love by what men might call "trifles." Although Frances is not a social activist like Julia, she fosters Julia's generalized maternity by eventually persuading Marianna to sell the house to Julia for the refuge she needs. In doing so, of course, Frances also nurtures the best aspects of Marianna's character. For herself, she savors the positive aspects of her middle years: "I am glad I am not so old as Cousin Adah because then I would be finished, and I am interested and want to go on; but I believe I am glad not to be as young as Maddie and this boy, who still have to do such a lot of making up their minds" (34).

Frances's mind may be made up, but it is not rigid; she has not remained a prey to ideologies like those that led to the Second World War.

> Frances [in her youth] had not long remained a Socialist. It was too all-settled, the air got a little stale, a room where you mustn't open the window; if you opened the window a breeze might come

in to disturb what was now all tidily arranged. A belief should be — nascent, more true this moment than ever before, because of this moment of newly discovered truth (14).

Although Glaspell presents her century of women in *Judd Rankin's Daughter*, much of the novel emphasizes the problems of a century of patriarchal ideologies. Frances must act as "a breeze" that will "disturb what was now all tidily arranged" in the minds of the men in her life, particularly her father and her biological and spiritual sons.

Frances's male relations are all sure of their convictions, but the variety of their beliefs is Glaspell's way of calling their certainty into question. Frances's father is an isolationist because he believes his son's death in the previous world war accomplished nothing (56–57). Her husband Len, a liberal literary critic, favors tolerance of diverse points of view, but he "disapproved of her thinking; he loved her but said her mind was undisciplined" (19). Their best friend Stephen Halsey is becoming increasingly drawn into the circle of a fascistic publisher, Fred Little. Their only son Judd idealistically went off to fight but has returned a bitter neurotic who blames his father's beliefs for the world's plight and tries to find a new father in Stephen Halsey and employment with Fred Little; he has swung from one ideological extreme to another.

In the usual pattern of Glaspell's late works, the heroine needs to find a spiritual son who would transmit the best of the past into the future since her male relations are inadequate and her daughter is incapacitated by gender restrictions. Frances does find such a son in Gerald Andrews, a young soldier whom she meets at Adah's deathbed. Gerald has come because he believes Adah has some special message about life to convey to him, but she is past speech by the time he reaches her. Frances inherits Adah's task, and, because her mind is "undisciplined," counsels him against ideologies, against relying too heavily on anyone's words: "What comes may be better than what was thought out. I think it is only when we surprise ourselves we can do anything for another" (39). Gerald dies, in contrast to the usual pattern of Glaspell's late works, and Frances is forced to find a way to transmit her beliefs in spontaneity and generosity through her biological son.

As Frances attempts to help young Judd, she also assists her father and husband. She manages to persuade her father to break his despondent silence and write to his grandson and namesake; whatever he told him causes young Judd to quit his job with Fred Little and start working in a war plant. Judd Rankin has broken out of his isolationist shell, Judd Mitchell is reclaimed for altruism, and Len Mitchell is reinforced in his liberalism and reunited with his son. On New Year's Eve, Frances contemplates this gathering of salvaged men.

> *Right this moment*, she thought; remember it always as it is this moment—so lovely here in our house tonight: the fire, candles, Mike [young Judson's dog], Len and her father, Judson *back*, and more than he had ever been before. Remember it; don't forget this moment when everything came right for us (252).

Through Frances's emphasis on remembering, the scene becomes what was "cherished and shared of old" even as it happens since such personal, familial happiness is necessarily transitory in a war-torn world; despite all her efforts, Frances can retain what she has achieved only in memory.

Earlier in the novel, Len had accused Frances of being an "isolationist" of "mother love" (115), but the ending proves otherwise. As Frances cherishes the pleasant firelit scene, she is called to the house of one of her neighbors who has just received word of her son's death in the war. In the last line, Frances enacts Glaspell's strong belief in nonbiological maternity: she leaves the personal happiness of her hearth and goes "out of her house, closing the door softly behind her" (254). In her lifetime, Glaspell has witnessed the situation of women inch forward and slide back; she has seen war and peace and then war again. Her faith in progress is diminished, but she clings to the hope that, though a good woman, a mother-figure like Frances, cannot change the world, she can alleviate its sufferings, elevate her own character, and keep a spark of hope alive for the future.

The problem is that Glaspell's unselfish heroines do not help themselves while helping other women, but are typically erased in favor of their male relations. In Glaspell's first novel, *The Glory of the Conquered*, Ernestine Hubers sacrifices her career for that of her husband; the nobility of soul she gains allows her to paint her masterwork after his death, a portrait of him. Katie Jones of *The Visioning* follows her new Socialist mate as she had previously followed her military father and brother. In *Bernice*, the title character uses her death to save her husband's soul. Naomi Kellogg of *Brook Evans* and Alison of *Alison's House* die after renouncing their brief taste of life in favor of their paternal names; their legacies will be transmitted to the future by spiritual sons. Irma Lee Shraeder of *Fugitive's Return* retreats to cultivate her own garden and leaves the action to her lover John Knight. The title character of *Norma Ashe* finds most of her life in ashes as a result of serving her husband's goals, but her ideals are transmitted to a spiritual son. Blossom Holt of *Ambrose Holt and Family*, Lydia Chippman of *The Morning Is Near Us*, and Frances Rankin Mitchell of *Judd Rankin's Daughter* all live for the sake of their sons, spiritual and biological, and, though they are the protagonists, they are erased from the titles of their books.

Throughout her work, Glaspell is fundamentally uncomfortable with women who seek autonomy, who attempt to be better by grasping what they need. Although she seems attracted by their courage, rebelliousness, and experimentation, Glaspell ultimately condemns them as selfish, as evidenced by the fates she assigns them: Minnie Wright of *Trifles* is imprisoned and possibly mad; Mrs. Patrick and Mrs. Mayo of *The Outside* are reclusive grotesques, Madeleine of *Inheritors* is headed for prison, and *The Verge*'s Claire Archer is insane.

Two figures emerge as potentially hopeful in Glaspell's works: the Woman from Idaho in *The People* and Ruth Holland of *Fidelity*. Both of these women have broken out of their stultifying lives and headed for the heady atmosphere of bohemian Greenwich Village. The difficulty is that Glaspell ends both narratives at that point. We do not see how or if they achieve autonomy. The Woman from Idaho's function as muse to the Editor of *The People* and Ruth's long years of service to her lover Stuart tell us only that they know how to sacrifice, not that they know how to live for themselves or ameliorate the condition of women.

As we turn into a new century, we may be discomfited by the fates of Glaspell's heroines and wish that she had written happier, more encouraging endings for them and for us. Susan Glaspell, however, though she is frequently called an idealist, is ultimately a realist in depicting the entrapments as well as the aspirations of a century of American women.

Notes

Introduction

1. Jane Tompkins, *Sensational Designs: The Cultural Work of American Fiction, 1790–1860* (New York: Oxford U P, 1985), xii.

2. Ezra Pound, "Hugh Selwyn Mauberley" in *Selected Poems of Ezra Pound* (New York: New Directions, 1956), 61–62.

3. Sandra M. Gilbert and Susan Gubar, *No Man's Land: The Place of the Woman Writer in the Twentieth Century. Volume I: The War of the Words* (New Haven: Yale U P, 1988), 21.

4. Gilbert and Gubar, title of chapter 1.

5. Dale Spender, *Mothers of the Novel: 100 Good Women Writers Before Jane Austen* (London: Pandora, 1986), 56.

6. For an analysis of today's "women's novel," see Janice A. Radway's *Reading the Romance: Women, Patriarchy, and Popular Literature* (Chapel Hill: U of North Carolina P, 1984), 84.

7. Quoted in Marcia Noe, "A Critical Biography of Susan Glaspell" (U of Iowa Ph.D., 1976), Ann Arbor: University Microfilms International, 1981, 164–65.

8. Arthur Hobson Quinn, *A History of the American Drama from the Civil War to the Present Day* (New York: F. S. Croft, 1943), 211–12.

9. Edna Kenton, "Provincetown and MacDougal Street," a memoir of Cook included in *Greek Coins: Poems by George Cram Cook* (New York: George H. Doran, 1925), 25.

10. Arthur and Barbara Gelb, *O'Neill* (New York: Harper & Row, 1960), 304.

11. Quoted in Noe, 3.

12. Ralph Waldo Emerson, "Self-Reliance" in *Selections from Ralph Waldo Emerson*, Stephen E. Whicher, ed. (Boston: Houghton Mifflin, 1957), 149.

13. "Nature" in *Selections from Ralph Waldo Emerson*, 56.

14. "Self-Reliance" in *Selections from Ralph Waldo Emerson*, 152.

15. "Self-Reliance," 150.

16. Nina Baym, *Woman's Fiction: A Guide to Novels by and about Women in America, 1820-1870* (Ithaca: Cornell U P, 1978), 11.

17. Baym, 17.

18. Baym, 39.

19. Baym, 20. Many of Baym's conclusions seem supported by another study of domestic fiction, Mary Kelley's *Private Woman, Public Stage: Literary Domesticity in Nineteenth-Century America* (New York: Oxford U P, 1984).

20. Susan Glaspell, *Fugitive's Return* (New York: Frederick A. Stokes, 1929), 324.

21. Marianne Hirsch has demonstrated that even as late as the 1970s, "it is the woman as *daughter* who occupies the center of the global reconstruction of subjectivity and subject-object relation." *The Mother/Daughter Plot: Narrative, Psychoanalysis, Feminism* (Bloomington: Indiana U P, 1989), 136.

22. For an extended discussion of French, and other, uses of the maternal metaphor, see Jane Silverman Van Buren, *The Modernist Madonna: Semiotics of the Maternal Metaphor* (Bloomington: Indiana U P, 1989). For a critique of the French feminist stress on the preoedipal, see Brenda O. Daly and Maureen T. Reddy's introduction to their edited volume, *Narrating Mothers: Theorizing Maternal Subjectivities* (Knoxville: U of Tennessee P, 1991), 1-18.

23. Sara Ruddick, "Maternal Thinking" in *Mothering: Essays in Feminist Perspective*, Joyce Trebilcot, ed. (Totowa, NJ: Rowman & Allanheld, 1984, 1983), 213-30. For the dangers as well as benefits of the maternal metaphor, see Nina Auerbach, "Artists and Mothers: A False Alliance," *Women and Literature*, 6 (1978): 3-15; and Susan Stanford Friedman, "Creativity and the Childbirth Metaphor: Gender Differences in Literary Discourse," *Feminist Studies*, 13 (1987): 49-82.

24. Susan Glaspell, *The Verge* in *Plays by Susan Glaspell*, C.W.E. Bigsby, ed. (Cambridge: Cambridge U P, 1987), 70. I am supplying the date of first production, not publication, for each play in this book.

25. Glaspell, *The Outside* in *Plays by Susan Glaspell*, 53.

26. Ruddick, 225, 217, 221.

Chapter 1

1. Martha Banta, *Imaging American Women: Idea and Ideals in Cultural History* (New York: Columbia U P, 1987), 553.

2. Marcia Noe writes that "Susan Glaspell's name does not appear in

the records of babies born on that day [July 1, 1882] in Scott County [Iowa]. However, the Scott County Census of 1880 lists a four-year-old Susie Glaspell, as well as a one-year-old Frank and a five-year-old Charles, as a member of Alice and Elmer's household at 502 Cedar Street [Davenport]. Drake University records indicate that Susan gave her age as twenty-one when she matriculated in the fall of 1897. Therefore it appears that Susan Glaspell was born in 1876, the year of America's Centennial celebration." In "A Critical Biography of Susan Glaspell" (University of Iowa, Ph.D., 1976), Ann Arbor: University Microfilms International, 1981, 11. For the biographical information in this chapter, I am greatly indebted to Noe's dissertation. I have also used Arthur E. Waterman's *Susan Glaspell* (New York: Twayne, 1966).

3. Susan Glaspell's Papers in the Berg Collection of the New York Public Library.

4. A 1932 Davenport newspaper quoted by Noe, 12.

5. Noe, 16.

6. Patricia Albjerg Graham, "Expansion and Exclusion: A History of Women in American Higher Education," *Signs: Journal of Women in Culture and Society*, 3 (1978): 761.

7. See, for example, *The Admission of Women to Universities: Testimony Gathered in Connection with an Essay in "The North American Review" for January 1883, on "University Education for Women"* (New York: S.W. Green's Son, 1883). Also see Carroll Smith-Rosenberg, "The New Woman as Androgyne: Social Disorder and Gender Crisis, 1870–1936" in her *Disorderly Conduct: Visions of Gender in Victorian America* (New York: Knopf, 1985), 245–96.

8. Smith-Rosenberg, "The New Woman as Androgyne" in *Disorderly Conduct*, 252.

9. Noe, 19–20.

10. Smith-Rosenberg, "Bourgeois Discourse in the Progressive Era" in *Disorderly Conduct*, 177.

11. Autobiographical sketch in the Berg Collection.

12. "'News Girl' on the Congress of Mothers," *Des Moines Daily News* (1 June 1900): 5.

13. Autobiographical sketch in the Berg Collection.

14. Rachel M. Brownstein, *Becoming a Heroine: Reading About Women in Novels* (New York: Viking, 1982), 294.

15. Quoted in Anne Commire, ed., *Yesterday's Authors of Books for Children* (Detroit: Gale Research, 1977), 125.

16. Hugh Dalziel Duncan, *The Rise of Chicago as a Literary Center from 1885 to 1920* (Totowa, NJ: Bedminster, 1964), 119.

17. Rosalind Rosenberg, *Beyond Separate Spheres: Intellectual Roots of Modern Feminism* (New Haven: Yale U P, 1982), 43–44.

18. "The Women of the University," *President's Report*, University of Chicago, 1902–1904, 110.

19. Noe, 37.

20. Susan Glaspell, *The Road to the Temple* (New York: Frederick A. Stokes, 1927, 1941), 193. Subsequent references to this work will be indicated within the text.

21. Philip Rappaport, *Looking Forward: A Treatise on the Status of Women and the Origin and Growth of the Family and the State* (Chicago: Charles H. Kerr, 1906), 12.

22. Charles H. Kerr, *What to Read on Socialism* (Chicago: Charles H. Kerr, [1906]), 22.

23. See Elizabeth K. Helsinger, Robin Lauterbach Sheets, and William Veeder; *The Woman Question: Defining Voices, 1837–1883* (New York: Garland, 1983), Vol. II; and Rosalind Rosenberg's *Beyond Separate Spheres*.

24. See Mark Pittenger, "Evolution, 'Woman's Nature,' and American Feminist Socialism, 1900–1915," *Radical History Review*, 36 (1986): 47–61.

25. Mari Jo Buhle, *Women and American Socialism, 1870–1920* (Urbana: U of Illinois P, 1981), 219. Also see John Buenker's "The New Politics" in *1915, the Cultural Moment: The New Politics, the New Woman, the New Psychology, the New Art and the New Theatre in America*, Adele Heller and Lois Rudnick, ed. (New Brunswick, NJ: Rutgers U P, 1991), 15–26.

26. May Wood Simons, *Women and the Social Question* (Chicago: Charles H. Kerr, 1899), 18.

27. G. Thomas Tanselle, "George Cram Cook and the Poetry of Living, with a Checklist," *Books at Iowa*, 24 (1976), 9.

28. Tanselle, 9. For more on Cook and Nietzsche, see Fred Matthews, "The New Psychology and American Drama" in *1915, the Cultural Moment*, 146–56.

29. Duncan, 157–58.

30. Quoted in Noe, 39.

31. Carolyn Heilbrun, *Writing a Woman's Life* (New York: Norton, 1988), 49.

32. Heilbrun, 50.

33. Floyd Dell, "A Seer in Iowa," in George Cram Cook's *Greek Coins* (New York: George H. Doran, 1925), 9.

34. Noe, 93.

35. Ellen Kay Trimberger notes that, influenced by European sexologists such as Edward Carpenter, the Greenwich Villagers still considered maternity woman's most valuable attribute, especially when applied to mothering one's mate. See "The New Woman and the New Sexuality: Conflict and Contradiction in the Writings and Lives of Mabel Dodge and Neith Boyce" in *1915, the Cultural Moment*, 108.

36. Dell in *Greek Coins*, 14.

37. See Helen Deutsch and Stella Hanau, *The Provincetown: A Story of the Theatre* (New York: Farrar & Rinehart, 1931); Robert Karoly Sarlos, *Jig Cook and the Provincetown Players: Theatre in Ferment* (U of Massachusetts P, 1982); Adele Heller, "The New Theatre"; and Mary C. Henderson, "Against Broadway: The Rise of the Art Theatre in America" (1900–1920) in *1915, the Cultural Moment*, 217–32, 233–49.

38. Autobiographical sketch in the Berg collection.

39. June Sochen, *The New Woman: Feminism in Greenwich Village, 1910–1920* (New York: Quadrangle, 1972), 5.

40. Henry D. Thoreau, *The Illustrated Walden*, J. Lyndon Shanley, ed. (Princeton: Princeton U P, 1973), 323.

41. Smith-Rosenberg, "The New Woman as Androgyne" in *Disorderly Conduct*, 282–83.

42. "The Oven Bird" in *The Poetry of Robert Frost*, Edward Connery Lathem, ed. (New York: Holt, Rinehart and Winston, 1969), 119.

43. Norman Matson, "The Shortest Way Out Was to the Left," *American Review*, 3 (1934): 488–53.

44. See the correspondence between Glaspell and Matson in the Berg Collection.

Chapter 2

1. Marcia Noe, "A Critical Biography of Susan Glaspell" (University of Iowa, Ph.D., 1976), Ann Arbor: University Microfilms International, 1981, 22.

2. "The Intrusion of the Personal," *Leslie's Monthly* (April 1904): 629–33; "For Tomorrow: The Story of an Easter Sermon," *Booklover's Magazine*, 5 (1905): 559–70.

3. *The Glory of the Conquered: The Story of a Great Love* (New York: Frederick A. Stokes, 1909). Subsequent references to this work will be indicated within the text.

4. "The Girl from Down-Town," *Youth's Companion*, 77 (1903): 160–61; "The Boycott on Caroline," *Youth's Companion*, 80 (1906): 137–39. Subsequent references to these stories will be indicated within the text.

5. "Contrary to Precedent," *Booklover's Magazine* (January–June 1904): 235–56. Subsequent references to this story will be indicated within the text.

6. Susan K. Harris, *19th-Century American Women's Novels: Interpretive Strategies* (Cambridge: Cambridge U P, 1990), 208.

7. Margaret Homans, *Bearing the Word: Language and Female Experience in Nineteenth-Century Women's Writing* (Chicago: U of Chicago P, 1986), 27.

152 *Notes*

8. "The Return of Rhoda," *Youth's Companion*, 79 (1905): 40; "At the Turn of the Road," *Speaker*, 2 (1906): 359–61; "For Love of the Hills," *The Black Cat*, 11 (1905): 1–11. Subsequent references to these stories will be indicated within the text.

9. "From A to Z," *American*, 65 (1909): 543. Due to the many magazines by this name, I was unable to locate the magazine version. I am quoting from the text in *Lifted Masks*, Glaspell's only collection of short fiction (New York: Frederick A. Stokes, 1912), 71–100. Subsequent references to this story will be indicated within the text.

10. Mary Kelley, *Private Woman, Public Stage: Literary Domesticity in Nineteenth-Century America* (New York: Oxford U P, 1984), 277.

11. Carroll Smith-Rosenberg, "The Hysterical Woman: Sex Roles and Role Conflict in Nineteenth-Century America" in *Disorderly Conduct: Visions of Gender in Victorian America* (New York: Knopf, 1985), 199.

12. Janice A. Radway, *Reading the Romance: Women, Patriarchy, and Popular Literature* (Chapel Hill: U of North Carolina P, 1984), 76.

13. Martha Banta, *Imaging American Woman: Idea and Ideals in Cultural History* (New York: Columbia U P, 1987), 366.

14. Elaine Showalter, ed. *These Modern Women: Autobiographical Essays from the Twenties* (Westbury, NY: Feminist Press, 1978), 5, 4.

15. Elizabeth Ammons, *Conflicting Stories: American Women Writers at the Turn into the Twentieth Century* (New York: Oxford U P, 1991), 10.

16. For more on Mercié's "Gloria Victis," see Peter Fusco and H.W. Janson, ed., *The Romantics to Rodin: French Nineteenth-Century Sculpture* (Los Angeles: Los Angeles County Museum of Art, 1980), 304–306.

17. "Catalogue of Works of Fritz Thaulow, A Loan Exhibition," Art Institute of Chicago, January 15 to January 28, 1903. I am indebted to Andrew Martinez, Assistant Archivist of the Art Institute, for the identification of Thaulow and a photocopy of the catalogue.

18. Myra Jehlen, quoted in Carolyn Heilbrun, *Writing a Woman's Life* (New York: Norton, 1988), 17.

19. In her dissertation, Noe emphasizes the importance of light imagery in Glaspell's fiction.

20. Nina Baym, *Woman's Fiction: A Guide to Novels by and about Women in America, 1820–1870* (Ithaca: Cornell U P, 1978), 36.

Chapter 3

1. Marcia Noe, "A Critical Biography of Susan Glaspell" (University of Iowa, Ph.D., 1976), Ann Arbor: University Microfilms International, 1981, 51.

2. Elizabeth Ammons, *Conflicting Stories: American Women Writ-*

ers at the Turn into the Twentieth Century (New York: Oxford U P, 1991), 5.

3. Quoted in Noe, 52.

4. Susan Glaspell, *The Visioning* (New York: Frederick A. Stokes, 1911), 19–20. Subsequent references to this novel will be indicated within the text.

5. Martha Banta, *Imaging American Women: Ideas and Ideals in Cultural History* (New York: Columbia U P, 1987), 553.

6. Mari Jo Buhle, *Women and American Socialism, 1870–1920* (Urbana: U of Illinois P, 1981), 106; Errol Wayne Stevens, "Heartland Socialism: The Socialist Party of America in Four Midwestern Communities, 1898–1920" (Indiana University, Ph.D., 1978), 25.

7. Noe notes the association of Ann with the dog, 55.

8. Joanne J. Meyerowitz, *Women Adrift: Independent Wage Earners in Chicago, 1880–1930* (Chicago: U of Chicago P, 1988).

9. Meyerowitz, 44.

10. Philip Rappaport, *Looking Forward: A Treatise on the Status of Women and the Origin and Growth of the Family and the State* (Chicago: Charles H. Kerr, 1906), 140.

11. Buhle, 266.

12. Deborah Silverton Rosenfelt, "Getting Into the Game: American Women Writers and the Radical Tradition," *Women's Studies International Forum*, 9 (1986): 368.

13. Charles H. Kerr, *What to Read on Socialism* (Chicago: Charles H. Kerr [1906]), 8.

14. Buhle, 290.

15. Dee Garrison, *Mary Heaton Vorse: The Life of an American Insurgent* (Philadelphia: Temple U P, 1989), 67. For a more detailed account, see Judith Schwarz, *Radical Feminists of Heterodoxy: Greenwich Village, 1912–1940* (Norwich, VT: New Victoria, 1986).

16. Susan Glaspell, *Fidelity* (Boston: Small, Maynard, 1915), 15. Subsequent references to this work will be indicated within the text.

17. Ann Ardis, *New Women, New Novels: Feminism and Early Modernism* (New Brunswick, NJ: Rutgers U P, 1990), 61.

18. One of Glaspell's short stories, published over a year before *Fidelity*, "The Rules of the Institution," has a similar situation, but, in contrast, one young woman cannot bring herself to advise another to obey "the rules of the institution." This short story has a number of parallels to *Fidelity*, both in theme and setting. *Harper's* 128 (1914): 198–208.

19. In one of Glaspell's short stories, "The Resurrection and the Life," published two years before *Fidelity*, the protagonist, Helen Freeman, has been deadened by her marriage in the same way both Ruth and Marion are in their relationship with Stuart. Also like Ruth and Marion, Helen

has an epiphany, but hers is largely unmotivated. *The Smart Set* (Sept. 1913): 65–68.

20. Carolyn G. Heilbrun, *Writing a Woman's Life* (New York: Norton, 1988), 130.

Chapter 4

1. I am providing the dates of the first production of each of Glaspell's plays, not their dates of publication.

2. I am not discussing Glaspell's collaborations with George Cram Cook, *Suppressed Desires* (1915) and *Tickless Time* (1918), or her collaboration with Norman Matson, *The Comic Artist* (1928), because of the difficulties of thematic attribution, nor do I examine the one-act farce *Close the Book* (1917) because it is so light and is not particularly relevant to an examination of women's roles. As part of my discussion of the revenge of the dutiful daughters in Chapter 7, I mention *Chains of Dew* (1922) when I discuss the novel into which Glaspell converted it, *Ambrose Holt and Family* (1931). *Alison's House* (1930) is treated in Chapter 6 with the other "ghostly" women of that period of Glaspell's writing.

3. Adrienne Rich, *Of Woman Born: Motherhood as Experience and Institution* (New York: Norton, 1986, 1976), xxxv.

4. Linda Ben-Zvi, "Susan Glaspell's Contributions to Contemporary Women Playwrights" in *Feminine Focus: The New Women Playwrights*, Enoch Brater, ed. (New York: Oxford U P, 1989), 152.

5. Susan Glaspell, "Contrary to Precedent," *Booklovers* (January–June 1904): 236.

6. Marcia Noe, "Susan Glaspell: A Critical Biography" (University of Iowa, Ph.D., 1976), Ann Arbor: University Microfilms International, 1981, 94. Robert K. Sarlos cites Ida Rauh, Edna St. Vincent Millay, Louise Bryant, and Eunice Tietjens as some of Cook's putative lovers and the sources of Glaspell's jealousy during the Provincetown days; "Jig Cook and Susan Glaspell: Rule Makers and Rule Breakers" in *1915, the Cultural Moment: The New Politics, the New Woman, the New Psychology, the New Art and the New Theatre in America*, Adele Heller and Lois Rudnick, ed. (New Brunswick, NJ: Rutgers U P, 1991), 258 n9. Ellen Kay Trimberger points out that free love worked more to the advantage of already culturally privileged Greenwich Village males and against women who preferred monogamy; "The New Woman and the New Sexuality: Conflict and Contradiction in the Writings and Lives of Mabel Dodge and Neith Boyce" in *1915, the Cultural Moment*, 105, 108.

7. Gayle Austin, *Feminist Theories for Dramatic Criticism* (Ann Arbor: U of Michigan P, 1990), 2.

8. The articles I found particularly helpful are: Karen Alkalay-Gut, "Jury of her Peers: The Importance of Trifles," *Studies in Short Fiction*, 21 (1984): 1–9; C.W.E. Bigsby, "Introduction" to *Plays* by Susan Glaspell (Cambridge: Cambridge U P, 1987), 9–12; Judith Fetterley, "Reading about Reading: 'A Jury of Her Peers,' 'The Murders in the Rue Morgue,' and 'The Yellow Wallpaper,'" in *Gender and Reading: Essays on Readers, Texts, and Contexts*, ed. Elizabeth A. Flynn and Patrocino P. Schweickart (Baltimore: Johns Hopkins U P, 1986): 147–64; Sharon P. Friedman, "Feminist Concerns in the Works of Four Twentieth-Century American Women Dramatists: Susan Glaspell, Rachel Crothers, Lillian Hellman, and Lorraine Hansberry" (New York University, Ph.D., 1977), Ann Arbor: University Microfilms International, 1977, 111–28; Annette Kolodny, "A Map for Rereading: Or, Gender and the Interpretation of Literary Texts," *New Literary History*, 11 (1980): 451–67; and Beverly A. Smith, "Women's Work — *Trifles*?: The Skill and Insights of Playwright Susan Glaspell," *International Journal of Women's Studies*, 5 (1982): 172–84. Glaspell later turned *Trifles* into a short story, "A Jury of Her Peers," *Everyweek* (March 5, 1917).

9. Beverly A. Smith argues that Minnie Wright may have been physically as well as emotionally battered. "Women's Work — *Trifles*?: The Skill and Insights of Playwright Susan Glaspell," *International Journal of Women's Studies*, 5 (1982): 172–84.

10. Susan Glaspell, *Trifles* in *Plays* (Boston: Small, Maynard, 1920), 25, 26. Subsequent references to this play will be indicated within the text.

11. Rich, 38.

12. Sharon P. Friedman, "Feminist Concerns in the Works of Four Twentieth-Century American Woman Dramatists: Susan Glaspell, Rachel Crothers, Lillian Hellman, and Lorraine Hansberry" (New York University, Ph.D., 1977), Ann Arbor: University Microfilms International, 1977, 124.

13. Annette Kolodny, "A Map for Rereading: Or, Gender and the Interpretation of Literary Texts," *New Literary History*, 11 (1980): 463.

14. C.W.E. Bigsby calls Mrs. Hale and Mrs. Peters' earlier neglect of Minnie Wright "a failure of sisterly solidarity." "Introduction" to *Plays* by Susan Glaspell (Cambridge: Cambridge U P, 1987), 11. The women's behavior is also an example of what Sara Ruddick finds one of the dangers of motherhood in a patriarchal, competitive society, that "a parent may feel compelled to preserve her *own* children, whatever befalls other children," or, in the case of *Trifles*, other women; "Maternal Thinking" in *Mothering: Essays in Feminist Theory*, Joyce Trebilcot, ed. (Totowa, NJ: Rowman and Allanheld, 1983, 1984), 217. Two more examples of exclusive mothering are Grandmother and Isabel Fejevary in Glaspell's *Inheritors*.

15. My supposition that Glaspell played roles that were particularly

significant to her is supported by the impression of the French director Jacques Copeau who saw her in *The People*:

> I observed on the stage a young woman of modest appearance, with a sensitive face, a tender and veiled voice. She was absolutely lacking in technique. She did not have the slightest notion of it. . . . And only at the end of her speech, she reached out her two arms simply, and she became suddenly silent, looking out straight ahead as if she was continuing to live her thoughts in the silence. Well, that gesture was admirable, and there was in that look a human emotion that brought tears to my eyes. I had a real woman before me, and the tears which she made me shed were not those involuntary tears brought on sometimes by the nervous excitement of the theater. They were real tears, natural tears, natural, human as she was.

Quoted in Noe, 103.

16. For the history and ideology of *The Masses*, see Eugene E. Leach, "The Radicals of *The Masses*" in *1915, the Cultural Moment*, 27–47.

17. Susan Glaspell, *The People* in *Plays* (Boston: Small, Maynard, 1920), 57. Subsequent references to this play will be indicated within the text.

18. The life-saving station was modeled upon the one in which Eugene O'Neill lived.

19. Susan Glaspell, *The Outside* in *Plays* (Boston: Small, Maynard, 1920), 109. Subsequent references to this play will be indicated within the text.

20. Ben-Zvi, 152.

21. *Woman's Honor* in *Plays* by Susan Glaspell (Boston: Small, Maynard, 1920), 124. Subsequent references to this play will be indicated within the text.

22. Christine Dymkowski, "On the Edge: the Plays of Susan Glaspell," *Modern Drama*, 31 (1988), 95.

23. Friedman, 148.

24. *Bernice* in *Plays* by Susan Glaspell (Boston: Small, Maynard, 1920), 176. Subsequent references to this play will be indicated within the text.

25. Noe, 108.

26. Friedman, 161. She also comments that "Glaspell, in this play, is clearly glorifying the power of insight and imagination over whatever necessary gains are made through political and social struggle" (161).

27. Bigsby, 16.

28. *The Road to the Temple* (New York: Frederick A. Stokes, 1927, 1941), 12. A genealogy in Glaspell's papers in the New York Public Library's Berg Collection indicates that the Mortons are partially modelled on Glaspell's own ancestors. In *The Road to the Temple*, Glaspell mentions the founding member of the Cook family in Iowa, Ira, and his friendship

with the Morton family (7). *The Road to the Temple* also provides another possible inspiration for *Inheritors*: Glaspell states that Cook wrote as story in which the "swing of the pendulum moves this family back and forth between idealism and materialism" (93–94) over the generations. The prototype of *Inheritors'* Grandmother appeared in Glaspell's one-act comedy *Close the Book* (produced in 1917; *Plays* [Boston: Small, Maynard, 1920], 63–96).

29. *Inheritors* in *Plays* by Susan Glaspell, C.W.E. Bigsby, ed. (Cambridge: Cambridge U P, 1987), 139. Subsequent references to this play will be indicated within the text.

30. *The Verge* in *Plays* by Susan Glaspell, C.W.E. Bigsby, ed. (Cambridge: Cambridge U P, 1987), 64. Subsequent references to this play will be indicated within the text.

31. J. Ellen Gainor also notes the identification of Claire with plants. "A Stage of Her Own: Susan Glaspell's *The Verge* and Women's Dramaturgy," *Journal of American Drama and Theatre*, 1 (1989): 84.

32. See Dymkowski, 95–96; 100–102.

33. Gainor presents a similar interpretation of Claire's relationship to her son by citing French feminist criticism: 91–92.

34. Rich, 193.

35. Ben-Zvi, 156.

Chapter 5

1. Quoted in Marcia Noe, "A Critical Biography of Susan Glaspell" (University of Iowa, Ph.D., 1976), Ann Arbor: University Microfilms International, 1981, 144.

2. "Dwellers on Parnassos," *New Republic* (17 January 1923): 198–200; "Last Days in Greece" in *Greek Coins: Poems by George Cram Cook with Memorabilia by Floyd Dell, Edna Kenton, and Susan Glaspell* (New York: George H. Doran, 1925), 31–49; "The Faithless Shepherd," *Cornhill Magazine*, 60 (1926): 51–69; *The Road to the Temple* (New York: Frederick A. Stokes, 1927, 1941). Subsequent references to these works will be indicated within the text.

3. Carolyn G. Heilbrun, *Writing a Woman's Life* (New York: Norton, 1988), 24.

4. Sidonie Smith, *A Poetics of Women's Autobiography: Marginality and the Fictions of Self-Representation* (Bloomington: Indiana U P, 1987), 55.

5. *Revealing Lives: Autobiography, Biography, and Gender*, Susan Groag Bell and Marilyn Yalom, ed. (Albany: State U of New York P, 1990), 4.

6. Floyd Dell, "A Seer in Iowa" in *Greek Coins*, 9.

7. Edna Kenton, "Provincetown and MacDougal Street" in *Greek Coins*, 25.

8. Ann Larabee has noted the Christ imagery with which Glaspell surrounds Cook in *The Road to the Temple*; "Death in Delphi: Susan Glaspell and the Companionate Marriage," *Mid-American Review*, 7 (1987): 95.

9. Bell and Yalom, 9. In the same volume, see Marilyn Yalom, "Biography as Autobiography: Adele Hugo: Witness of Her Husband's Life," 53–63; and Carol Hanberry MacKay, "Biography as Reflected Autobiography: The Self-Creation of Anne Thackeray Ritchie," 65–79.

10. See Noe, 143.

11. Heilbrun, 12.

12. For various responses to *The Road to the Temple*, see *New Statesman*, 28 (February 5, 1927): 510–11; the *Times Literary Supplement* (November 18, 1926): 811; Joseph Collins, *New York Evening Post Literary Review* (April 2, 1927): 2; Rosamond Guilder, "Spring Freshets: The Season's Theatre Books," *Theatre Arts Monthly*, 11 (1927): 377; Larabee, op. cit.; William Jordan Rapp, *The Independent*, 118 (April 9, 1927): 394, 396; and Arthur E. Waterman, *Susan Glaspell* (New York: Twayne, 1966), 51.

13. I take the term "life history" from *Interpreting Women's Lives: Feminist Theories and Personal Narratives*, Personal Narratives Group, ed. (Bloomington: Indiana U P, 1989), 4.

14. Estelle C. Jelinek, *The Tradition of Women's Autobiography: From Antiquity to the Present* (Boston: Twayne, 1986), xiii.

15. Jelinek, 25.

16. Jelinek, 44–45.

17. Bella Brodzki and Celeste Schenck, "Introduction" to *Life/Lines: Theorizing Women's Autobiography* (Ithaca: Cornell U P, 1988), 11.

18. Noe, 153.

19. Larabee, 95.

20. Larabee, 105.

Chapter 6

1. Elaine Showalter, ed. *These Modern Women: Autobiographical Essays from the Twenties* (Westbury, NY: The Feminist Press, 1978), 9–10: "The collapse of the suffrage coalition, the factionalization of the women's movement into bitterly opposed parties, and the absence of a clearly defined female voting bloc contributed to the political decline. On the personal level, the difficulty of applying feminist theory to daily life in a society still organized on patriarchal principles, and the younger genera-

tion's disavowal of the ideals and goals of the women's movement, led to fatigue and withdrawal among former leaders."

2. Lynette Carpenter and Wendy K. Kolmar, ed. *Haunting the House of Fiction: Feminist Perspectives on Ghost Stories by American Women.* (Knoxville: U of Tennessee P, 1991), 18, 12, 16, 1.

3. *Brook Evans* (London: Victor Gollancz, 1928, 1929), 37. Subsequent references to this novel will be indicated within the text.

4. Adrienne Rich, *Of Woman Born: Motherhood as Experience and Institution* (New York: Norton, 1986, 1976), 61.

5. Arthur E. Waterman has pointed out the parallel with Norman Matson in *Susan Glaspell* (New York: Twayne, 1966), 95–96.

6. Judith Arcana, *Every Mother's Son* (Garden City, NY: Anchor/Doubleday, 1983), viii.

7. Carol Gilligan, *In a Different Voice: Psychological Theory and Women's Development* (Cambridge: Harvard U P, 1982), 74.

8. *Fugitive's Return* (New York: Frederick A. Stokes, 1929), 18, 25. Subsequent references to this novel will be indicated within the text.

9. Gilligan, 74.

10. Gilligan, 74, 105.

11. For more on the Dickinson-Stanhope parallels, see Waterman, 86–87; Marcia Noe, "A Critical Biography of Susan Glaspell" (University of Iowa, Ph.D., 1976), Ann Arbor: University Microfilms International, 1981, 175; and Gerhard Bach, *Susan Glaspell und die Provincetown Players* (Frankfurt: Peter D. Lang, 1979), 188–89. I like to think that Glaspell would have quoted Dickinson's "'Houses'—so the Wise Men tell me—" if she had had the permission of the Dickinson estate since the poem concerns the unfulfilled promises of the house of the patriarchy: Number 127 in *The Complete Poems of Emily Dickinson*, Thomas H. Johnson, ed. (Boston: Little, Brown, 1960), 59.

12. *Alison's House* (New York: Samuel French, 1930). Subsequent references to this play will also be indicated within the text.

13. Critics generally dislike *Alison's House* because it is a "well-made play" and so a retreat from Glaspell's experimental Provincetown plays; for an excellent assessment along these lines, see C.W.E. Bigsby's "Introduction" to *Plays* by Susan Glaspell (Cambridge: Cambridge U P, 1987), 26–29. Cynthia Sutherland argues that the play is a thematic retreat in that it "safely distanced controversial feminist issues by presenting women tethered by Edwardian proprieties rather than more immediately recognizable topical restraints"; "American Women Playwrights as Mediators of the 'Woman Problem,'" *Modern Drama*, 21 (1978): 330. I am taking Sutherland's argument a step further to assert that *Alison's House* represents a surrender, not just a retreat, in the context of Glaspell's other works of the late 1920s.

14. Sandra M. Gilbert and Susan Gubar, *No Man's Land: The Place of the Woman Writer in the Twentieth Century*. Volume I: *The War of the Words* (New Haven: Yale U P, 1988), 182.

Chapter 7

1. Maggie Lane, *Literary Daughters* (London: Robert Hale, 1989), 11.

2. Marcia Noe, "A Critical Biography of Susan Glaspell" (University of Iowa, Ph.D., 1976), Ann Arbor: University Microfilms International, 1981, 172. She also provides an analysis of *Chains of Dew*, 127-31.

3. *Ambrose Holt and Family* (New York: Frederick A. Stokes, 1931), 2. Subsequent references to this novel will be indicated within the text.

4. Carolyn G. Heilbrun, *Writing a Woman's Life* (New York: Norton, 1988), 18.

5. Arthur E. Waterman, *Susan Glaspell* (New York: Twayne, 1966), 100.

6. Lynda Zwinger, *Daughters, Fathers, and the Novel: The Sentimental Romance of Heterosexuality* (Madison: U of Wisconsin P, 1991), 3. Also see Linda Gupta, "Fathers and Daughters in Women's Novels" (American University, Ph.D., 1983), Ann Arbor: University Microfilms International, 1983.

7. Blossom's plight illustrates two of the temptations that Sara Ruddick believes beset mothers under a patriarchy, the tendency to cherish one's own children at the expense of other children and the desire to raise socially acceptable children: "Maternal Thinking" in *Mothering: Essays in Feminist Theory*, Joyce Trebilcot, ed. (Totowa, NJ: Rowman & Allanheld, 1983, 1984), 217, 221.

8. *Alison's House* (New York: Samuel French, 1930), 150.

9. Waterman, 101.

10. Waterman, 107.

11. I am indebted to Marcia Noe for biographical information about this decade, 190-200.

12. *The Morning Is Near Us* (New York: Frederick A. Stokes, 1939, 1940), 3. Subsequent references to this novel will be indicated within the text.

13. Noe, 210.

Chapter 8

1. In the 1940s, Glaspell also wrote a play, "Springs Eternal," which she was unable to have produced. In "A Critical Biography of Susan Glaspell," Marcia Noe observes that "'Springs Eternal' is supposed to be a

World War II comedy, but tired jokes about the Red Cross, gasoline rationing, and extramarital affairs do little to relieve its tedium"; (University of Iowa, Ph.D., 1976), Ann Arbor: University Microfilms International, 1981, 224.

2. Barbara Frey Waxman, *From the Hearth to the Open Road: A Feminist Study of Aging in Contemporary Literature* (New York: Greenwood, 1990), 2.

3. Waxman, 17.

4. The epigraph to *Cherished and Shared of Old* reads "life best," but in George Cram Cook's "From Sappho," the phrase is "life's best." *Greek Coins* (New York: George H. Doran, 1925), 140. The change or error is intriguing since Cook's version chooses only a part of life while Glaspell's epigraph embraces all of life.

5. *Cherished and Shared of Old* (New York: Julian Messner, 1940), no pagination.

6. *Norma Ashe* (New York: Lippincott, 1942), 56. Subsequent references to this novel will be indicated within the text.

7. Norma Ashe illustrates three of what Sara Ruddick believes are the temptations to mothers in patriarchal society: cherishing her own children over other children, "fearfulness and excessive control," and the desire to raise socially acceptable children: "Maternal Thinking" in *Mothering: Essays in Feminist Theory*, Joyce Trebilcot, ed. (Totowa, NJ: Rowman & Allanheld, 1983, 1984), 216, 217, 221.

8. Waxman, 19.

9. *Judd Rankin's Daughter* (New York: Grosset & Dunlap, 1945), 19. Subsequent references to this novel will be indicated within the text. This description of Frances could also apply to photographs of Glaspell in middle age.

Index

Pages in italics refer to major discussion.